SAFE SCHOOLS SAFE FUTURES

Preventing Violence, Bullying, and Harassment with the Critical Aggression Prevention System (CAPS)

Dr. John D. Byrnes

Center for Aggression Management, Inc.

Dedication

To all the remarkable individuals who have joined me on this 30-year adventure—your presence, support, and contributions have been invaluable. If you know me, you know my definition of an adventure: when you take a challenge and add risk, that's when the adventure truly begins. Risk is not a gamble—it's a calculation. So, calculate well, but never shy away from the adventure.

As Joseph Campbell might have said, this has been more than just a journey—it's been a hero's journey. And for that, I am forever grateful. You know who you are.

Copyright Page

SAFE SCHOOLS, SAFE FUTURES

Preventing Violence, Bullying, and Harassment with the

Critical Aggression Prevention System (CAPS)

Copyright © 2024 by Dr. John D. Byrnes

All rights reserved.

No part of this book may be reproduced, stored in a retrieval system, or transmitted in any form or by any means, without the prior written permission of the author, except for brief quotations in a book review.

The following phrases are the property of John D. Byrnes: Aggression Management®, Aggression Manager™, Aggression Continuum™, Primal & Cognitive Aggression Continua™, Unmagnificent Seven™,

ISBN: 979-8-218-51785-4

Printed in the United States of America

NOTE:

Interested in Mastering Aggression Prevention?

If you're looking to gain comprehensive training in identifying and preventing aggression, consider enrolling in our **Aggression First Observers' Online Course** and **Certified Aggression Managers' Online Course**. These courses offer the knowledge and tools for early identification and prevention of aggression.

To get started, simply contact us:

- **Phone**: (407) 718-5637
- **Email**: info@AggressionManagement.com

Upon completion of the Certified Aggression Managers' Course, you'll receive a **Certificate of Completion** from the Center for Aggression Management, Inc.

Contents

Preface 1
    SAFE SCHOOLS, SAFE FUTURES

Chapter 1 3
    THE CRISIS OF SCHOOL VIOLENCE AND THE NEED FOR PREVENTION

Chapter 2 9
    THE AGGRESSION CONTINUUM AND ITS IMPORTANCE IN SCHOOLS

Chapter 3 15
    THE ROLE OF AGGRESSION FIRST OBSERVERS

Chapter 4 23
    CERTIFIED AGGRESSION MANAGERS: DIFFUSING AND REDIRECTING AGGRESSION

Chapter 5 31
    RECOGNIZING AGGRESSION AT EVERY STAGE

Chapter 6 41
    TRUST: THE FOUNDATION OF PREVENTION AND PERSUASION

Chapter 7 47
    PREVENTING SEXUAL HARASSMENT, BULLYING, AND DISCRIMINATION BEFORE THEY START

Chapter 8 55
    CRISIS PHASE: MANAGING HIGH-RISK AGGRESSION

Chapter 9 61
    THE SCIENCE BEHIND CAPS: PREVENTING AGGRESSION WITH SCIENTIFIC RELIABILITY

Chapter 10 69
    ADAPTING CAPS TO DIFFERENT ENVIRONMENTS: SCHOOLS, WORKPLACES, AND HEALTHCARE

Chapter 11 77
ONGOING TRAINING AND PROFESSIONAL DEVELOPMENT WITH CAPS

Chapter 12 83
INTEGRATING CAPS INTO BROADER ORGANIZATIONAL SAFETY STRATEGIES

Chapter 13 89
THE FUTURE OF CAPS: EVOLVING TO MEET NEW CHALLENGES

Chapter 14 95
COLLABORATING WITH MENTAL HEALTH PROFESSIONALS: A HOLISTIC APPROACH TO AGGRESSION PREVENTION

Chapter 15 101
CAPS INNOVATION: NEW TOOLS AND TECHNOLOGIES FOR THE FUTURE

Chapter 16 109
FOSTERING LONG-TERM BEHAVIORAL CHANGE AND ORGANIZATIONAL CULTURE WITH CAPS

Chapter 17 115
MEASURABLE OUTCOMES: THE IMPACT OF CAPS ON SAFETY, WELL-BEING, AND PRODUCTIVITY

Chapter 18 121
THE FUTURE OF CAPS: ADAPTING TO A RAPIDLY CHANGING WORLD

Chapter 19 127
IMPLEMENTING CAPS FOR LONG-TERM SUCCESS: A GUIDE FOR ORGANIZATIONS & INSTITUTIONS

Chapter 20 133
CULMINATION – CAPS: A COMPREHENSIVE SYSTEM FOR A SAFER FUTURE

Chapter 21 147
THE ANATOMY OF A SCHOOL SHOOTER

This page intentionally left blank

Preface

SAFE SCHOOLS, SAFE FUTURES

The future of our children—our greatest treasure—is inseparably linked to the safety they experience today. As parents, grandparents, and, for me, as a new great-grandparent, we know that nothing is more essential than ensuring a safe environment where they can grow, learn, and thrive. The title *Safe Schools, Safe Futures* speaks to more than just the immediate need for safer schools; it embodies a vision for a future where every child, every family, and every community can flourish in a world free from the threats of aggression and violence. By protecting our children in schools, we're not merely safeguarding their present—we're investing in their future and the future of society itself.

We see the disruption on college campuses across the nation today. By helping children create a safe space in our secondary schools, we are not only protecting them now but also equipping them with the tools to stay safe when they eventually reach colleges and universities. This focus on aggression prevention during their formative years lays the groundwork for a lifetime of security, enabling them to navigate even the most challenging environments with confidence.

This book shines a light on the profound impact that creating safer schools has on the next generation, equipping them to navigate the complexities of the world with confidence and security. Through a focus on aggression prevention and the cultivation of a culture of safety, we are laying the foundation for a future filled with potential. Our children—embodying our hopes, dreams, and aspirations—deserve a future that is not only secure but brimming with opportunity. The insights shared here aim to help turn that vision into a reality.

In today's fast-paced world, rising aggression in schools, workplaces, and communities poses an escalating threat. Over my three decades in aggression prevention, I've witnessed how the early identification of precursors to aggressive behavior can prevent tragic incidents, reduce associated costs, and most importantly, save lives. The lives saved could be those of our children, grandchildren, or, as in my case, great-grandchildren. This book is my response to the growing need for preventive solutions. I firmly believe that aggression can be managed—if not entirely prevented—through early detection and timely intervention.

The 19 chapters that follow are designed to provide you with practical tools for addressing aggression before it escalates into violence. Whether you're a school principal, business manager, HR professional, or security expert, the strategies presented here will help you recognize the precursors to aggression and take swift action to prevent harm. My goal in writing this book is simple: to offer a preventive solution where traditional approaches remain reactive. Together, we can prevent incidents before they occur, protect the innocent from becoming victims, stop aggressors before they become perpetrators, and save organizations significant costs.

Thank you for joining me on this journey. Together, we can make our schools, workplaces, and communities safer for the future we envision for our children.

Sincerely,

Dr. John D. Byrnes

Founder, Center for Aggression Management, Inc.

Interested in Mastering Aggression Prevention?

If you're looking to gain comprehensive training in identifying and preventing aggression, consider enrolling in our Aggression First Observers' Online Course and Certified Aggression Managers' Online Course. These courses offer the knowledge and tools for early identification and prevention of aggression.

To get started, simply contact us:

- Phone: (407) 718-5637
- Email: info@AggressionManagement.com

Upon completion of the Certified Aggression Managers' Course, you'll receive a Certificate of Completion from the Center for Aggression Management, Inc.

Chapter 1

THE CRISIS OF SCHOOL VIOLENCE AND THE NEED FOR PREVENTION

Our students, our children, are our greatest treasure. As a parent, a grandparent, and recently a great-grandparent, I believe we must do everything possible to protect our children in our schools. These institutions, which act as surrogate parents under the doctrine of *in loco parentis*, are entrusted with the care and safety of our children. Yet, despite this immense responsibility, our schools often fall short in protecting our most vulnerable.

Today, schools are merely reacting to incidents of sexual harassment, abuse, bullying, discrimination, and violent behavior—addressing the damage only after it has occurred. Think about this: Doesn't "Bullying" represent someone exhibiting bullying behavior? This reactive approach, while well-intentioned, comes far too late. By the time a school intervenes, there is already a victim, a perpetrator, and sometimes an entire community shaken by the trauma. The lives of both victims and aggressors, whether physically harmed or not, are often permanently scarred, emotionally and psychologically. This is unacceptable, and it must stop now!

We must shift our focus from reacting to violence to preventing it. Schools can no longer afford to wait until an incident occurs before taking action. This book will show how we can end this reactive, disgraceful approach to violence in our schools and introduce a new path forward—one that ensures the safety of our children through proactive and reliable prevention.

As someone who deeply cares about the safety of students and educators, I feel compelled to address the growing crisis of school violence in the United States. Once a rare and unthinkable occurrence, acts of violence—ranging from bullying to devastating mass shootings—are now alarmingly common. These incidents leave emotional, psychological, and sometimes physical scars that can take years to heal. More importantly, many of these tragedies could have been prevented if we had the right tools in place. The time for change is now.

The Escalating Threat of School Violence

School shootings are the most extreme and visible form of school violence, and they have devastated communities across the U.S. According to the Gun Violence Archive, there were 34 school shootings in 2021—a shocking rise from previous years. The trauma left behind from these tragedies doesn't just impact the victims but ripples through entire communities, leaving emotional devastation in its wake.

Take, for example, the massacre at Sandy Hook Elementary School in December 2012, where 26 people were killed, including 20 children. The shooter had displayed signs of aggression and mental health issues for years, yet no effective intervention took place. If a system like CAPS (Critical Aggression Prevention System) had been in place to identify the early stages of his escalating aggression, lives might have been saved. School shootings, while the most catastrophic, aren't the only form of aggression. Bullying, physical fights, and psychological torment happen every day in schools across the country. And without a preventive system like CAPS, these behaviors often go unchecked until it's too late.

The horrific reality is that schools are acting only after the damage is done. We are failing our children by not taking proactive steps to stop violence before it escalates. CAPS can identify the early precursor-signs of someone *"on the path to violence"* and intervene before it escalates—offering a **scientifically reliable approach** to ensuring our children's safety, one that is desperately needed.

Let me emphasize the critical need to prevent violence rather than merely react to it. The "Moment of Commitment" is the instant an assailant decides to pull the trigger. From that decision to the first shot being fired, is only 2 seconds. No security measures, no School Resource Officer (SRO), no matter how well-trained or equipped, can reliably respond in just 2 seconds. I confirmed this with the Director of Operations at NASRO (National Association of School Resource Officers), who unequivocally stated, "Absolutely not!"

What happens after those 2 seconds? When the SRO arrives, they do what they've been trained to do—step over the dead, dying, and wounded to reach the shooter. While I understand the protocol, it's unacceptable to me. We must intervene before this horrific "Moment of Commitment," so as to prevent this incident and with CAPS, we can.

Bullying and Its Far-Reaching Effects

Bullying, often seen as less severe than shootings, can have long-term, devastating consequences. The National Center for Education Statistics reports that 20% of students between the ages of 12 and 18 are bullied during the school year. Today, cyberbullying has made it even harder for students to escape harassment, often following them home through social media and other online platforms.

Consider the case of Phoebe Prince, a 15-year-old high school student from Massachusetts, who took her own life in 2010 after months of relentless bullying. Despite complaints from her family, the school failed to take effective action. With a system like CAPS, the early precursor-signs of her distress could have been identified and addressed before tragedy struck. CAPS provides a scientifically reliable approach to recognizing early aggression, which could have made all the difference for Phoebe and countless others. We must ask ourselves; how many more children must suffer before we make a change?

The Impact on Mental Health Assessments

The rise in school violence goes hand in hand with a mental health crisis among young people. According to the National Alliance on Mental Illness, 1 in 6 youth experiences a mental health disorder each year. Mental health struggles often manifest as aggression, leading to verbal outbursts, physical altercations, or worse. We cannot afford to ignore these warning signs.

In the Columbine High School shooting in 1999, both shooters exhibited troubling behavior long before the massacre. Yet, without a system like CAPS, there was no reliable way to track and address these early precursor-signs. The current system relies too much on subjective assessments and reactive measures—tools that time and time again fail to prevent tragedy. CAPS, by contrast, focuses on identifying the pre-incident precursors to violence, offering a reliable way to intervene early—before it's too late.

Chapter 1

Traditional mental health assessments, while essential for diagnosing disorders, have shown significant limitations in predicting future violence. These evaluations are often subjective and notoriously inaccurate. Take, for example, the case of Nikolas Cruz, the Parkland shooter, who underwent evaluation and was deemed not at risk of harming himself or others—tragically, this assessment was incorrect, and 17 innocent lives were lost as a result. The reliance on such subjective assessments played a role in this devastating outcome.

Similarly, after the Virginia Tech massacre, where 32 faculty members and students were killed, it was revealed that the shooter, Seung-Hui Cho, had been assessed three separate times. Each assessment diagnosed him as depressed and anxious but concluded he posed no risk of harming himself or others. These tragic events highlight the inherent weaknesses of conventional mental health evaluations in identifying potential violence.

In the case of Jared Lee Loughner, who shot Congresswoman Gabrielle Giffords and killed six others, he exhibited clear signs of a thought disorder, likely schizophrenia—one of the more potentially dangerous mental illnesses. However, it is crucial to recognize that only *Two-Tenths of One Percent* of individuals with schizophrenia commit murder. How can we predict who, among this tiny fraction, will become violent? The truth is, we can't—not with traditional methods.

The Critical Aggression Prevention System (CAPS) offers a solution by focusing on identifying early behavioral precursors to violence. Unlike subjective mental health assessments, CAPS provides scientifically reliable and privacy-compliant interventions, enabling early, objective prevention before violence occurs.

Social media has compounded these issues. Today's youth are more connected than ever before, and with that connection comes an increase in online harassment and bullying. According to the Pew Research Center, 59% of U.S. teens have experienced some form of online harassment. Mallory Grossman, a 12-year-old from New Jersey, tragically took her own life in 2017 after relentless cyberbullying. Despite her family's pleas, the school failed to intervene. Had CAPS been in place, the early warning signs of her distress could have been identified, allowing for intervention before the situation became fatal. The stakes are too high for us to continue relying on outdated, reactive systems.

The Emotional Toll on Students and Teachers

Violence and aggression in schools don't just impact those directly involved. The emotional and psychological effects ripple through the entire school community. Students who witness or experience violence often suffer from long-term mental health issues. According to the American Psychological Association, exposure to school violence can lead to anxiety, depression, and even PTSD. And it's not just the students who bear the burden. Teachers, who are often on the front lines of these incidents, report feeling overwhelmed and unsupported. A survey by the American Federation of Teachers found that 78% of teachers feel physically and emotionally unsafe in their school environment.

CAPS not only helps to prevent violence but also serves as a tool to support teachers and create a safer learning environment for everyone. By using data to track and address early precursor-signs of aggression, CAPS reduces the pressure on educators, giving them the tools they need to identify problems early and provide appropriate interventions.

The Need for a Proactive (Preventive) Solution: Introducing CAPS

It's clear that traditional approaches to school violence—lockdown drills, school resource officers (SROs), and reactive interventions—are not enough. These methods react to violence after it has already occurred, offering little in the way of prevention. What if we could prevent these incidents from happening in the first place? What if we could stop the bullying, harassment, and violence before they begin? This is exactly what CAPS offers.

CAPS is a scientifically reliable, data-driven system designed to identify early warning signs of aggression and intervene before the behavior escalates into violence. Unlike other systems that rely on subjective assessments, CAPS uses measurable data to track behaviors and provide schools with actionable insights. This allows educators to intervene early, before a situation spirals out of control, and provide the necessary support to at-risk students. Most importantly, CAPS does this while remaining fully compliant with privacy regulations like HIPAA and FERPA, ensuring the safety of our children without infringing on their privacy.

Chapter 1

As a parent, grandparent, and great-grandparent, I know the value of protecting our children. I care deeply about creating safer schools, and I believe CAPS is the tool that can make this vision a reality. There are school districts that are actually discussing arming their teachers, but the real solution is to equip everyone with CAPS.

In the chapters ahead, I will show you how CAPS works, why it is essential for preventing school violence, and how we can implement this system to build safer, more supportive learning environments for all students. We must act now—because our children, our greatest treasure, deserve nothing less.

Chapter 2

The Aggression Continuum and Its Importance in Schools

As educators, administrators, and staff committed to preventing violence in schools, it's essential to understand that aggression is rarely spontaneous. It follows a predictable and measurable path, moving through distinct phases before reaching a critical crisis point. Recognizing and intervening early in this process can dramatically change outcomes. The earlier we engage, the easier it becomes to de-escalate and diffuse potentially harmful situations.

At the heart of the **Critical Aggression Prevention System (CAPS)** is the **Aggression Continuum**, a scientifically reliable tool that allows schools to identify the early precursor-signs of aggression and intervene before they escalate into violent or destructive behavior. The continuum helps schools move from a reactive posture—responding only after an incident has occurred—to a proactive one, preventing harmful behavior before it even begins.

The **Aggression Continuum (Also known as the Primal & Cognitive Aggression Continua)** is similar to the FBI's framework of "identifying someone on the path to violence." However, we go a step further by focusing on what we call the **"sequential successive precursors to violence."** These precursors allow us not only to prevent violence but also to address and prevent issues like **sexual harassment**, **abuse**, **bullying**, **discrimination**, and **assaultive behavior** long before they develop into a crisis. By identifying these precursors, CAPS enables schools to take swift, appropriate action at the earliest stages of aggression, preventing both physical and emotional harm to students and staff.

The Aggression Continuum: A Predictable Path

The **Aggression Continuum** consists of a series of phases that aggressive behavior typically follows. These phases move from **Trigger Phase**, where aggression is more subtle, to the **Escalation Phase**, where behavior intensifies, and finally to the **Crisis Phase**, where aggressive actions become overt and dangerous.

It's important to recognize that aggression doesn't emerge suddenly—it builds over time. Our Aggression Continuum helps us identify aggressive behaviors early, long before they escalate into incidents like bullying. By intervening at these early stages, we can apply the appropriate skills to maximize the chances of diffusing the situation effectively.

Most people only recognize aggression once it reaches an obvious point, such as two people shouting at each other—that's actually Stage 6 on our continuum. However, there are many subtle acts of aggression that occur well before this point. Through training, we equip you to spot these early warning signs, engage proactively, and prevent incidents from escalating into bullying.

Additionally, our system allows us to monitor behavior shifts and address them before they escalate into crises. By training educators and school staff to recognize where a student's behavior falls on the continuum, we provide them with the tools to intervene early, preventing conflict and fostering a safer environment.

Why Schools Need Early Intervention

Traditional school safety programs, such as lockdown drills and response to active shooters, are valuable but ultimately **reactive**. These programs address threats **after** they've materialized. Let's face it, "Run, Hide, Fights" is not a prevention strategy! Students and teachers are already being murdered! But with CAPS, we aim to shift from reaction to **prevention**.

Early intervention has profound implications for schools:

- It reduces the likelihood of violence, saving lives.
- It prevents incidents of bullying, sexual harassment, discrimination, and abuse.
- It fosters a healthier, safer school environment, where students feel supported, respected, while enhancing student achievement.

When schools can spot aggression in its **Trigger Phase**, they can stop the behavior before it spirals into something much more dangerous. This is where CAPS stands apart from traditional programs. We will expand on this later in this book.

The Importance of Addressing All Forms of Aggression

The **Aggression Continuum** addresses both **Primal** and **Cognitive Aggression**, ensuring that schools can identify and manage aggression in all its forms. **Notice the color coding and labeling:** green for low risk, yellow for moderate risk, and red for high risk.

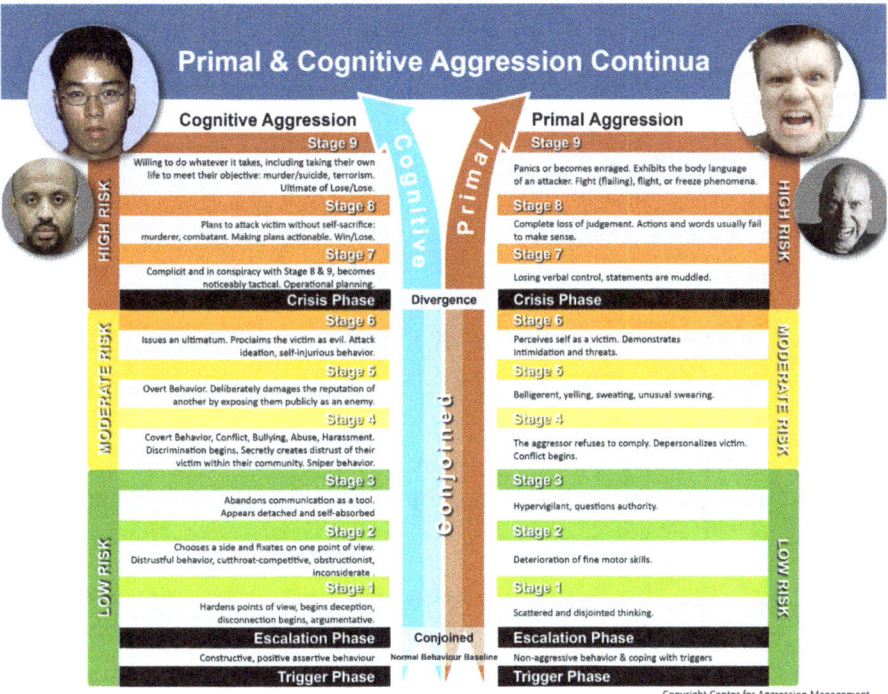

- **Primal Aggression**: This type of aggression is driven by adrenaline. Often described as **Primal Instinct**—a fight-or-flight response fueled by adrenaline due to emotions like fear, anger, or frustration. It's often impulsive and reactive, hard to control but generally short-lived. For example, a student might lash out verbally or physically when feeling threatened, even if they don't fully understand why.

- **Cognitive Aggression**: In contrast, cognitive aggression is intent-driven and thus more **calculated and deliberate**. This is the **intent to do harm to another**. It involves planning, manipulation, and an intent to achieve specific outcomes. While primal aggression is impulsive, cognitive aggression is strategic, and it can be much more difficult to detect because it often hides behind rational behavior. A student who quietly undermines a peer by spreading rumors or exclusion is an example of cognitive aggression.

Both forms of aggression can lead to harmful outcomes if left unchecked, but they require different approaches for prevention and management. **We will expand on our Primal & Cognitive Aggression Continua later in this book.** The **Aggression Continuum** helps schools identify which type of aggression is driving a student's behavior, ensuring the right intervention strategy is applied.

How CAPS Helps Schools Stay Ahead of Violence

At its core, CAPS provides schools with a framework to be **out in front of violence**. By understanding the stages of the Aggression Continuum and equipping school staff with the ability to recognize and respond to early precursor-signs of aggression, we move away from crisis management and toward proactive intervention.

CAPS allows schools to:

- **Spot precursor-warning signs** of aggression incidents in students.
- **Identify the type of aggression**—whether it's primal or cognitive—that's driving a student's behavior.
- **Implement corresponding interventions** that prevent aggression from escalating into an incident.

It's not just about preventing violence. CAPS gives schools the tools to prevent harmful behaviors like bullying, harassment, and discrimination. By understanding aggression on this deeper level, educators can create environments where students feel safe and supported, which improves both their academic achievement and social success.

Real-World Example: Early Intervention Saves the Day

Imagine a situation where a high school student, James, begins withdrawing from social activities, displaying irritability and frustration over small issues. In many schools, this behavior might go unnoticed until it worsens. But in a CAPS-equipped school, this is recognized as a **Trigger Phase behavior** within the Baseline of the Aggression Continuum and James is not coping, thus he is about to enter Stage One of our Aggression Continuum.

A **First Observer**, trained through CAPS, logs this behavior into the system. This action alerts a **Certified Aggression Manager** (CAM), who steps in to assess the situation. After meeting with James, the CAM discovers that he's been experiencing significant stress at home, leading to his emotional distress. The CAM works with James to redirect his frustrations in a healthier, more productive way, preventing further escalation. We discuss these "convincing" strategies in more detail later in this book.

Without CAPS, James might have gone unnoticed until his behavior reached the **Crisis Phase**, where his frustration could have led to a physical altercation or other violent outbursts. But with early intervention, the school prevented the situation from escalating, keeping both James and his classmates safe.

Conclusion: Why Understanding the Aggression Continuum Matters

The **Aggression Continuum** gives schools the roadmap to recognize aggression before it spirals into violence. By understanding how aggression progresses and learning to identify it early, schools can **prevent incidents** from happening, rather than simply reacting to them after the fact.

In the following chapters, we'll dive deeper into the specific roles of **Aggression First Observers** and **Certified Aggression Managers** and how they contribute to this layered approach. Together, these roles create a proactive and reliable system for preventing aggression and maintaining a safe learning environment for students.

This page intentionally left blank

Chapter 3

THE ROLE OF AGGRESSION FIRST OBSERVERS

In the desire to prevent violence, harassment, bullying, and other harmful behaviors in schools, the role of the **Aggression First Observer (AFO)** is vital. Although we have had occasions where employers wanted all employees to have all skills, most want a two-tiered training system. These individuals are the first line of defense in identifying the early precursor-signs of aggression and taking action before it escalates. Trained to spot the subtle cues that may otherwise go unnoticed, Aggression First Observers serve as the eyes and ears on the ground, equipped to recognize the precursor signs that indicate a student is moving along the Aggression Continuum.

While other safety measures in schools focus on responding to violence after it occurs, **Aggression First Observers** are proactive. They don't wait for an incident to unfold—they work to prevent it from happening in the first place.

What is an Aggression First Observer?

An **Aggression First Observer** (AFO) is any individual within the school community who has been trained to recognize the early precursor signs of aggression. This role can be filled by **teachers, coaches, counselors, staff members, bus drivers (who are the first observer the students), security personnel**, or **school resource officers (SROs)**. These individuals are not necessarily specialists in behavior or psychology; rather, they are trained to observe, identify, and report early precursor-signs of aggressive behavior.

AFOs play a critical role in CAPS by providing the essential **first step** in the intervention process. By spotting the early precursor-signs of both **Primal** and **Cognitive Aggression**, they help prevent situations from escalating into an incident of bullying, abuse, sexual harassment, discrimination, as well as violence or severe emotional harm.

Chapter 3

Training for Aggression First Observers

The training for AFOs is designed to be practical and accessible. It equips school personnel with the knowledge and skills to identify the **precursors** of aggression, even in its earliest stages. AFOs are taught to understand the **Aggression Continuum** and recognize the behavioral indicators of both **Primal** and **Cognitive Aggression**.

Key components of AFO training include:

- **Recognizing Primal Aggression:** Primal aggression is fueled by the body's release of adrenaline, creating a direct link between heightened stress and observable aggressive behaviors. This physiological response isn't just something we observe—it's measurable. During my work with the military, we used infrared technology to remotely monitor a person's pulse rate from just a square inch of skin. By watching their pulse rise or fall in response to stimuli, we gathered valuable data. This is not theory—it's hard science.

  Aggression First Observers (AFOs) are trained to detect the early precursor-signs of primal aggression, such as scattered, disjointed behavior, changes in body language, and visible signs of stress. For instance, a student showing these early indicators, which align with Stage 1 on the Primal Aggression Continuum may be dealing with significant frustration, irritability, or physical tension from challenges at home.

  By recognizing these signs early and engaging the student in a genuine, caring manner, you can build rapport and trust, helping to defuse the situation before it escalates. This proactive approach allows you to divert potential incidents and create a safer, more supportive environment.

- **Detecting Cognitive Aggression**: Cognitive aggression is intent-driven—the calculated desire to harm others. Unlike primal aggression, it is often more subtle, cloaked in rational or seemingly innocuous behavior. Too often, people are blindsided by this type of aggression, but we have the only scalable system that reliably identifies and reports on Cognitive (intent-driven) Aggression.

AFOs are trained to spot manipulative or strategically harmful actions that signal the intent to cause emotional, social, or psychological damage. The first step is distinguishing between **assertive** and **aggressive** behavior. Assertive behavior is constructive—it's about striving to be the best version of oneself, while aggressive behavior is destructive, focused on winning by "taking others down." Aggression, in any form, is always negative and harmful, whereas assertiveness fosters positive outcomes. Assertive behavior represents the **Cognitive Aggression Continuum's Baseline** and upon entering the Stage 1 of this continuum, the person now exhibits **aggressive** behavior.

Cognitive aggression can manifest in various ways: passive-aggressive remarks, efforts to undermine trust, withdrawing from relationships, exclusionary behavior, or subtle forms of intimidation. Detecting these early precursor-signs of aggression is critical in preventing further escalation and maintaining a safe, healthy environment.

- **Behavioral Observation**: AFOs learn how to observe behavior in the classroom, hallways, playgrounds, and other school environments. This includes looking for patterns of withdrawal, irritability, or social isolation that may indicate a student is in distress or moving along the Aggression Continuum.

- **Effective Reporting**: One of the most critical aspects of an AFO's role is reporting. AFOs are taught how to document both aggressive behavior, logistics, and report their observations in a timely and accurate manner, ensuring that a trained **Certified Aggression Managers (CAMs)** can take appropriate action.

Recognizing Early Precursors of Aggression

The earlier a sign of aggression is recognized, the more effective the intervention will be. Aggression doesn't begin at the Crisis Phase—it builds from subtle behaviors in the **Trigger Phase,** from **those who are coping with these triggers** and **those who are not coping** and thus enter into the **Escalation Phase at Stage 1 with scattered and disjointed thinking**. AFOs are trained to spot these behaviors before they become obvious, which gives schools the chance to intervene early and prevent more serious incidents.

Early Subtle Precursor-Signs of Primal Aggression:

- Communication appears scattered and disjointed
- Physical signs of distress (verbalizing slight anger, frustration and/or discomfort).
- Inability to cope with minor frustrations (e.g., difficulty with assignments or peer interactions).
- Disproportionate responses to challenges or perceived threats.
- Inexplicable misconduct or questioning authority

For example, if a student reacts aggressively to a minor inconvenience, such as losing a game at recess, it may indicate they are in the **Trigger Phase of aggression and not coping**, which corresponds to Stage 1 of the Primal Aggression Continuum. Recognizing these early behaviors allows the AFO to intervene by providing support, diffusing the situation. This proactive approach helps diffuse potential escalation and prevents the situation from worsening.

Subtle Early precursor-signs of Cognitive Aggression:

- Transitioning from assertive behavior to aggressive behavior
- Moving from mutually beneficial behavior to looking out only for oneself to the determent of others
- Passive-aggressive comments or subtle insults aimed at peers.
- Manipulative behavior that is designed to gain control or influence over others.
- Exclusionary tactics (e.g., excluding someone from social groups).

Identifying Personalities That Are Inconsiderate or Harmful to Others: These behaviors often manifest in individuals whose actions naturally create victims. Whether through a lack of empathy, manipulative tactics, or aggressive tendencies, these personalities can be damaging to those around them, leading to emotional, social, or psychological harm.

Recognizing these traits early allows for timely intervention, helping to protect potential victims and address the underlying issues.

Cognitive Aggression can be more difficult to detect because it's often cloaked in seemingly rational behavior. AFOs are trained to look beyond the surface and recognize when a student is using calculated actions to undermine others. Early detection of Cognitive Aggression is critical because it can prevent serious emotional or psychological harm, as well as stop conflicts from escalating into violence.

How Aggression First Observers Work with Certified Aggression Managers

While Aggression First Observers are responsible for identifying and reporting early precursor-signs of aggression, they are not tasked with resolving the situation entirely on their own. This is where **Certified Aggression Managers (CAMs)** come in. Once an AFO identifies a student who is showing signs of Primal or Cognitive Aggression, they report their observations to a CAM through a CAPS Dashboard. More on this latter.

The **two-tiered approach** ensures that each situation is handled with the appropriate level of expertise. AFOs provide the early warning system, while CAMs—who are trained in more advanced strategies for de-escalation and redirection—take over to assess the situation and implement the necessary interventions. CAMs are individuals who have gone through our one-day online training AFO's training: 7 to 8 hour and then a second-day online training to become a Certified Aggression Manager.

This collaboration is crucial for creating a seamless and preventive system that allows schools to prevent incidents of aggression from occurring. By working together, AFOs and CAMs can effectively manage aggressive behavior at every stage of the continuum.

Case Study: The Importance of Early Observation

Example 1: Spotting the Precursors of Primal Aggression

Mrs. Stevens, a teacher at a middle school, had just completed her AFO training when she noticed that one of her students, Alex, appeared

Chapter 3

scattered and disjointed this morning, plus he seemed to be unusually irritable for several days. He had begun snapping at classmates over minor things, like who sat in his favorite seat or who borrowed his pencil. These were small incidents, but they stood out to Mrs. Stevens because Alex was typically calm and cooperative.

Recognizing these behaviors as potential precursors to Primal Aggression, Mrs. Stevens logged the incident into the CAPS Mobile App, which immediately updated the CAPS system. This alert was instantly processed through the CAPS Dashboard, notifying the school's Certified Aggression Managers (CAMs). The school's CAMs are trained to respond to these alerts generated by the CAPS Dashboard so as to inform the Administrator if they have knowledge helpful to the Administrator, whether about Alex or the circumstances surrounding this case.

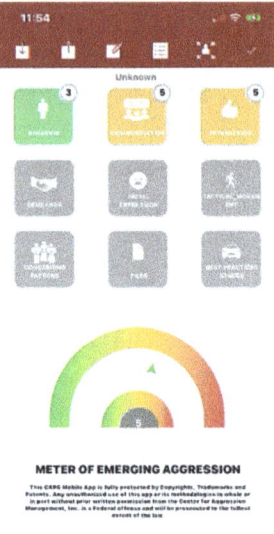

After receiving input from the CAMs, the Administrator assigned one or more Certified Aggression Managers to engage with Alex, assess his situation, and begin the diffusing and

redirection process. The CAMs then report back to the Dashboard

Administrator with key information: What did they observe? How did they respond? What were the outcomes?

This is a scientific process. While a single case doesn't establish validation, when patterns are observed across 50, 500, or even 5,000 cases, the data builds a solid foundation for validation that can withstand rigorous scrutiny.

They discovered that Alex had been dealing with issues at home, causing his frustration to boil over at school. Early intervention and counselling prevented Alex from escalating to more aggressive or harmful behavior.

Example 2: Detecting Cognitive Aggression

Mr. Jones, an AFO-trained bus driver, noticed that one of the students, Sarah, had been making passive-aggressive comments to a fellow student, Amy, for several days. Sarah was polite when speaking to teachers and appeared well-behaved, but Mr. Jones could tell that her comments to Amy were designed to undermine her. After Sarah's behavior continued, Mr. Jones reported it through the CAPS system.

A **Certified Aggression Manager** stepped in, recognizing Sarah's actions as early precursor-signs of **Cognitive Aggression**. They worked with Sarah to address the root of her behavior, preventing it from escalating into outright bullying or social exclusion. Without Mr. Jones's early observation, this situation could have escalated, potentially causing emotional harm to Amy.

Conclusion: A Proactive First Line of Defense

Although there are employers who want all of their employees to be trained as Certified Aggression Managers, most want a two-tiered system of training. To this end, Aggression First Observers are the foundation of the CAPS system. By equipping school personnel with the ability to identify the early precursor-signs of aggression, CAPS empowers schools to intervene before aggression escalates into more serious conflicts. AFOs are essential in maintaining a safe, supportive school environment by catching aggression early and ensuring it is addressed before it becomes a problem.

In the next chapter, we'll explore the advanced role of **Certified Aggression Managers (CAMs)** and how they work to de-escalate and redirect aggression, using persuasion and redirection techniques to guide students toward more constructive outcomes.

This page intentionally left blank

Chapter 4
CERTIFIED AGGRESSION MANAGERS: DIFFUSING AND REDIRECTING AGGRESSION

While Aggression First Observers (AFOs) are crucial in identifying early warning signs of aggression, it is the Certified Aggression Managers (CAMs) who step in to manage, de-escalate, and redirect that aggression. CAMs are equipped with advanced training that enables them to assess both the aggressor's underlying intent and the trajectory of their current behavior. They understand that "humans tend to act in what they believe is their best interest," and are skilled in redirecting the aggressor's Intentions.

How? By demonstrating that the current path the aggressor is on leads to negative consequences, the CAM offers an alternative solution—one that addresses the aggressor's concerns but without the same harmful outcomes. If the CAM can effectively convince the aggressor that this new path aligns more closely with their interests, the individual will choose to follow it, motivated by their own intentions.

This intervention not only redirects the aggressor's behavior but also prevents any potential violent incident that may have occurred had they stayed on their original path. The data collected will show that the CAM successfully averted a violent incident, contributing to real-time, evidence-based best practices.

In this chapter, we'll explore the role of Certified Aggression Managers in the **Critical Aggression Prevention System (CAPS)**, their methods for managing both **Primal** and **Cognitive Aggression**, and how they go beyond mere de-escalation to **redirect** aggression in a way that benefits both the aggressor and the school community.

What Is a Certified Aggression Manager (CAM)?

A **Certified Aggression Manager (CAM)** is someone trained in advanced techniques to manage, diffuse, and redirect aggression in both **Primal** and **Cognitive Aggression**. CAMs are not only responsible for de-escalating situations but also for understanding the intentions that drive aggressive behavior and provide an alternatives path (redirect) that aligns with the aggressor's goals in a positive and productive manner. This is redirection, and if the aggressor is convinced effectively the CAM can demonstrate in real-time that he or she have prevented any subsequent violence by their redirection illustrating evidence-based best practices.

The CAM role is critical in the CAPS system because, while AFOs are responsible for early detection, CAMs handle the **more complex task** of managing aggression once it has been identified. This two-tiered approach ensures that schools can intervene at every level of the Aggression Continuum, addressing both the **emotional (adrenaline-driven)** and **strategic (intent-driven)** aspects of aggressive behavior.

Managing Primal vs. Cognitive Aggression

A key aspect of a CAM's role is recognizing whether aggression is driven by **Primal** or **Cognitive** forces and tailoring their approach accordingly.

Primal Aggression: Adrenaline-Driven (Emotional and Instinctive)

Primal Aggression is first and foremost adrenaline-driven, it is often reactive, emotional, and triggered by threat, fear, anger, or frustration. It is based on the brain's **fight, flight, or Freeze response** and tends to be impulsive. In these situations, the aggressor's emotions have taken over, leading to potentially destructive actions.

A CAM's role in managing **Primal Aggression** involves:

- **Calming the Situation by Helping the Aggressor Regain Emotional Control:** Certified Aggression Managers (CAMs) are trained in techniques, including Navy SEAL breathing exercises, to help them maintain their own composure during tense situations. When engaging with an aggressor whose adrenaline levels are already elevated, it's natural for the CAM's own adrenaline to rise in response, preparing the body for potential conflict. However, this can unintentionally escalate the aggression.

This is why CAMs are trained to stay calm under pressure. Calm is contagious, and by maintaining a composed demeanor, CAMs can model the emotional control needed to diffuse the situation. By staying calm, they create a ripple effect, helping the aggressor regain control over their own emotions, which is crucial in de-escalating the potential for violence.

- Using **de-escalation techniques**, such as active listening and calm body language, to create a non-threatening environment where the aggressor can feel safe and understood. The CAM can now begin developing rapport and subsequently trust. We train CAMs in the skills to gender trust.

- Redirecting the emotional energy by offering alternative, more constructive ways for the aggressor to express their feelings.

For example, if a student lashes out during class because they feel threatened or overwhelmed, a CAM would first through modeling work to calm the student down, acknowledging their emotions and helping them regain emotional control. Then, the CAM would guide the student toward a solution-focused conversation, perhaps encouraging them to express their frustrations through dialogue or problem-solving rather than outbursts.

Cognitive Aggression: Calculated and Intent-Driven

In contrast, **Cognitive Aggression** is more deliberate and calculated. The aggressor acts with intent, often with a specific goal in mind—whether it's to dominate a social situation, undermine a peer, or achieve personal gain at someone else's expense. **Cognitive Aggression** is less about emotions running high and more about intent-driven strategic actions that can be hidden behind seemingly rational behavior.

Managing **Cognitive Aggression** requires a different approach:

- **Assessing the intent** behind the aggressor's actions. CAMs need to understand what the aggressor is trying to achieve and why they believe their current behavior will help them reach their goal.

- Demonstrating to the aggressor that their current strategy is flawed and will likely lead to **significant negative consequences**.

- Offering a **better, more constructive path** that still aligns with the aggressor's underlying needs or goals but in a way that doesn't harm others or escalate conflict.

It's crucial to understand that an aggressor is not purely a **Primal Aggressor** or a **Cognitive Aggressor**—they are often a combination of both. For example, if I, as an inconsiderate person, say something that offends you, you immediate response is a spike in adrenaline—this is **Primal Aggression**. However, when I choose to follow up taking action against you, that's **intent-driven** or **Cognitive Aggression**.

When I then choose to act against you, that decision is driven by **Cognitive Aggression**. As you can see, these two types of aggression feed into one another, escalating the situation until it potentially reaches a **crisis phase**. Recognizing how primal and cognitive elements interplay is key to diffusing aggression before it escalates further. CAMs are trained to identify whether this aggressor is driven more by Primal or Cognitive Aggression. This is important because CAMs must approach Primal and Cognitive Aggression differently.

For example, if a student is bullying a peer to elevate their social status, the CAM would recognize this as primarily Cognitive Aggression, where the behavior is **driven by an intent to do harm,** calculated and intentional. The CAM would then help the aggressor understand that while the bullying may provide a short-term boost in status or power, it will inevitably result in negative long-term consequences, such as social isolation or disciplinary actions. Once the student realizes that this behavior is not in their best interest, the CAM can guide them toward more constructive ways of building relationships and influence—such as excelling in group projects or offering support to peers. This approach helps redirect the student's behavior toward positive, socially constructive alternatives. **Once achieved this CAM has prevented any subsequent aggressive incidents from this aggressor.**

In contrast, if the aggressor's behavior is driven more by Primal Aggression, the CAM's first objective should be to remove the source of the aggressor's anxiety. Calming the immediate emotional response will allow the CAM to engage with the student more effectively before addressing longer-term solutions. **Remembering the typically the aggressor will be effected by both Primal and Cognitive Aggression.**

The Power of Redirection: Offering a Better Path

A core function of a **Certified Aggression Manager** is not just to diffuse aggression but to **redirect** it. Redirection involves helping the aggressor realize that the path they are currently on—whether driven by primal emotions or cognitive intent—is not in their best interest. CAMs achieve this by offering an **alternative path** that is not only constructive but also helps the aggressor meet their underlying needs in a more constructive and positive way.

Understanding Human Intention

A key premise behind the CAM's approach is that **humans tend to do what they believe is in their best interest**. By understanding the aggressor's Intentions, CAMs can convince them that their current actions will not serve their long-term goals. Instead of forcing the aggressor to back down, CAMs present them with a **better option**—one that is aligned with their interests but does not harm others or escalate the situation.

This is especially important in managing **Cognitive Aggression**, where the aggressor often believes they are acting rationally and strategically. CAMs use their training to:

- **Persuade the aggressor** that their strategy will ultimately fail or bring unwanted consequences.
- Offer a more **constructive solution** that still addresses the aggressor's goals but in a way that promotes collaboration, respect, and mutual benefit.

Real-World Example: Redirecting Primal and Cognitive Aggression

Consider the case of a high school student, Jordan, who was lashing out at classmates during group activities. Initially, this behavior appeared to be **Primal Aggression**—Jordan was clearly frustrated and overwhelmed by the dynamics of the group. A CAM intervened and helped Jordan regain control of his emotions, encouraging him to use **calm communication** to express his concerns rather than lashing out. This de-escalation prevented the situation from worsening, and Jordan returned to the group with a calmer mindset. The CAM may actually practice his Navy Seal's breathing techniques with this aggressor aiding Jordan to find his calm.

However, upon further assessment, the CAM realized that Jordan's behavior also had an element of **Cognitive Aggression**. He was using his emotional outbursts to manipulate the group into doing things his way, dominating discussions, and undermining others. The CAM addressed this by showing Jordan that while his current strategy gave him short-term control, it was alienating him from his peers and would likely backfire in the long run. Instead, the CAM worked with Jordan to develop better leadership skills, encouraging him to collaborate with others and gain respect through **positive contributions** rather than aggression.

Going Beyond Diffusion: The CAM's Role in Long-Term Behavioral Change

Certified Aggression Managers (CAMs) are not merely conflict diffusers—they are **behavioral shapers**. Their role extends far beyond de-escalating aggressive incidents. CAMs work closely with aggressors to foster long-term behavioral change, ensuring that students not only calm down in the moment but also develop the skills to manage their emotions and interactions more effectively in the future.

All interventions and progress are meticulously tracked and monitored through the **fully forensic CAPS Dashboard**. Importantly, CAPS operates in full compliance with privacy regulations, including **HIPAA** (which governs medical records), **FERPA** (which safeguards school records), and the **Civil Rights Act of 1964**. This ensures that school districts can record and track aggressive behavior with confidence, knowing they are adhering to legal standards while effectively managing student behavior. We have found that school district's legal counsel are very pleased with the use of CAPS training and CAPS Dashboard because all of the information gathered, including actions taken, are done so in a clear, concise and formal way.

CAMs accomplish this by:

- **Identifying triggers** that lead to aggressive behavior and helping the aggressor understand how to cope with these triggers in healthier ways.
- **Developing communication and problem-solving skills** that allow the aggressor to navigate conflicts without resorting to aggression.

- **Monitoring progress** and offering ongoing support to ensure the aggressor is following the new, more constructive path.

The goal is not just to prevent aggression in the short term but to equip students with the tools they need to succeed in the long run, both in school and in life.

Conclusion: Certified Aggression Managers as Agents of Positive Change

Certified Aggression Managers (CAMs) are essential to the success of the CAPS system. They are not only responsible for preventing violent or aggressive incidents—they are instrumental in **redirecting aggression** toward more positive outcomes. By understanding the deeper Intentions behind both Primal and Cognitive Aggression and offering better alternatives, CAMs guide students away from destructive behaviors and toward personal growth.

Certified Aggression Managers (CAMs) typically serve as part of a Threat Assessment Team or Behavioral Intervention Team, but they also work within a multidisciplinary team. Often, these teams include mental health professionals who, while bound by privacy regulations and unable to discuss specific mental health diagnoses, can actively participate in discussions around "aggressive behavior". This collaboration is particularly powerful because it ensures that everyone on the team is using the same language and operating under a unified framework.

By standardizing how aggressive behavior is identified and managed, CAMs and their teams ensure that schools and campuses can truly claim to be "as safe as possible"—the highest standard of evidence-based Best Practices. This consistency across disciplines makes it possible to proactively address threats while maintaining compliance with privacy regulations.

In the next chapter, we will delve deeper into the **Aggression Continuum** itself, exploring each stage in detail and examining how aggression progresses from minor emotional responses to serious confrontations. Understanding these stages is critical to preventing escalation and maintaining a safe, supportive school environment.

This page intentionally left blank

Chapter 5
RECOGNIZING AGGRESSION AT EVERY STAGE

The **Aggression Continuum** is a core concept within the **Critical Aggression Prevention System (CAPS)** that helps schools identify, manage, and prevent aggression before it escalates into violence or other harmful behaviors. Aggression doesn't appear out of nowhere—it follows a predictable path, moving from subtle emotional responses in its early stages to more overt and dangerous actions if left unchecked. Understanding the stages of aggression and recognizing the signs at each phase is key to successful early intervention.

In this chapter, we'll take a closer look at each stage of the Aggression Continuum and how schools can intervene at the right moments to prevent escalation. By identifying these behaviors early, schools can stop aggression in its tracks, ensuring a safer environment for both students and staff.

The Aggression Continuum: From Trigger to Crisis

The Aggression Continuum is divided into three main phases: **Trigger**, **Escalation**, and **Crisis**. Each phase represents a distinct progression in the development of aggressive behavior, and within each phase, specific stages highlight key moments for intervention. The earlier we can detect signs of aggression, the more effectively we can prevent harmful outcomes.

1. The Trigger Phase: Early precursor-signs of Aggression

The **Trigger Phase** is the baseline prior to entering the Primal Aggression Continuum's Stage 1 level of aggression. As long as individuals are coping with these triggers, everything is copasetic. When they stop coping, this is when they enter Stage 1 of the Primal Aggression Continuum and where aggression begins to develop, often with subtle scattered and disjointed thinking. This is the earliest signs of aggression where you might witness a student who seems unusually tongue-tied or whose fine motor skills, like writing, seem to be imparted. This is the most critical time for intervention because it's when aggressive behaviors are easiest to redirect.

Signs of someone not copying with their Triggers: Primal Aggression: Escalating emotional responses such as irritability, frustration, or sudden low level emotional outbursts that are disproportionate to the situation. These are often short-lived but can signal a deeper, underlying issue.

In contrast to the Primal Aggression Continuum, the Cognitive Aggression Continuum represents a shift from assertive behavior toward aggressive behavior. This transition involves subtle changes, where behavior moves from mutually beneficial actions to self-serving ones that can harm others. These intent-driven behaviors—such as passive-aggressive comments, manipulation, or excluding others—are often covert and more strategic in nature.

At this stage, Cognitive Aggression is frequently rooted in personality flaws, like the example of an "inconsiderate person" who doesn't perceive themselves as an aggressor, yet their actions are creating victims, making them, in fact, an aggressor. Cognitive aggression often manifests through calculated actions aimed at exerting control or causing harm, while maintaining an outward appearance of rational behavior. This level of aggression can be particularly harmful due to its subtlety, making it essential to identify and address early.

Example of the Trigger Phase:

Johnny, a middle school student, arrives at school late and is already feeling frustrated. He didn't have breakfast, missed the bus, and had a tense argument with his mother that morning. As the day progresses, Johnny snaps at a classmate over a small issue in the lunch line. This irritability and frustration are early precursor-signs of **Primal Aggression**—he is reacting emotionally to the stress he's experienced throughout the day.

In this scenario, a trained **Aggression First Observer (AFO)** could recognize Johnny's behavior as an early precursor to aggression. By reporting this behavior on his CAPS Mobile App, a CAM can quickly intervene and offer support, the CAM can prevent Johnny's frustration from escalating into a more serious incident later in the day. Because Johnny is now in the CAPS Dashboard, the Administrator will now follow up with Johnny to see that he continues to cope with daily triggers and thus not escalate into the Primal Aggression Continuum. In this scenario, a trained Aggression First Observer (AFO) recognizes Johnny's behavior as an early precursor to aggression. By promptly reporting the behavior through the **CAPS Mobile App,** a **Certified Aggression Manager (CAM)** can intervene early, providing support to prevent Johnny's frustration from escalating into a more serious incident later in the day. Now that Johnny's behavior is logged in the **CAPS Dashboard**, the Administrator can monitor his progress, ensuring that he continues to cope with daily triggers and does not escalate into the Primal Aggression Continuum.

2. The Escalation Phase: Aggression Begins to Intensify (Stages 1 through 6):

The Escalation Phase (Stages 1-3)

The **Escalation Phase**, which encompasses **Stages 1-3 (Low Risk)**, represents a critical shift where changes in behavior, body language, and communication patterns become evident. These early stages often reveal personality traits that create victims, offering opportunities for timely intervention. In our courses, we identify what we call the **Unmagnificent Seven Personalities** as **The Sherman Tank, The Sniper, The Exploder, The Complainer, The Negativist, The Clam,** and **The Bulldozer**—individuals who display behaviors that harm others, whether they recognize it or not. For instance, **inconsiderate people** may not see themselves as aggressors, but their actions create victims, making them aggressors, nonetheless.

While some of these behaviors bleed into Stages 4-6 as the aggression intensifies, they begin in Stages 1-3, rooted in personality flaws that, if unchecked, escalate into more destructive forms of aggression.

Signs of the Escalation Phase Stage 1-3:
- **Primal Aggression**: At this stage, triggers have accumulated to the point where the individual's coping mechanisms are overwhelmed. Their emotional and cognitive control diminishes, making their aggression more visible. The individual may show signs of mounting tension, signaling an increased likelihood of conflict.

The key takeaway is that **early identification and intervention** are crucial when dealing with a **Primal Aggressor**. The sooner you recognize and engage with them, the easier it is to diffuse and redirect their behavior. As the aggressor escalates, they progressively lose the ability to make sound judgments, making it harder for them to control their actions and for you to effectively intervene. This loss of control not only increases the risk of conflict but also diminishes your ability to convince them to change course.

- **Cognitive Aggression**: In this Stages 1-3, behaviors become increasingly uncooperative, nonproductive, and detached. The individual may demonstrate a lack of empathy, start creating distance from others, and engage in deceptive actions to conceal their aggression. Then individuals start exhibiting "distrustful" behavior, they tend to fixate on their own ideas, disregarding others; they lack responsibility and conscience. Then the appear detached and self-absorbed.

Example of the Escalation Phase:

Jane, a high school student, has been making passive-aggressive comments toward her peer, Joan, for several weeks. Initially, Jane's behavior was subtle, but it has now escalated to more overt manipulation, such as spreading rumors about Joan and intentionally excluding her from social activities. This behavior represents **Cognitive Aggression** that is becoming more intense and calculated, as Jane's actions are aimed at harming Joan's social standing.

At this point, a **Certified Aggression Manager (CAM)** can intervene to address Jane's behavior. While Jane's actions may offer her short-term social gains, the CAM will demonstrate how these behaviors will ultimately lead to negative consequences, such as damaged relationships and social isolation. The CAM can present Jane with alternative strategies to achieve her social goals without harming others, thus diffusing the situation before it escalates further.

Signs of the Escalation Phase Stage 4-6 (Moderate Risk):

In **Stage 4**, the aggressor often engages in **covert actions** intended to undermine the victim's trust relationships within their **community**. Here, "community" refers to the individuals the victim likes, loves, and respects, and with whom they seek mutual trust and respect. The aggressor subtly sows doubt within the community, perhaps by saying something like, "I don't know about Joan anymore. I can't explain it, but I just don't trust her like I used to." This seemingly innocent remark can spread quickly, eroding trust and creating division within the community like wildfire.

In **Stage 5**, the aggressor moves from covert to overt actions, openly casting the victim **as an enemy of their own community**. This shift is marked by the aggressor actively working to turn the community against the victim, solidifying the divide and increasing the victim's social isolation.

In **Stage 6**, the aggressor escalates further by portraying Joan as the ultimate enemy of her community, **branding her as "evil."** At this point, the aggressor's actions turn the community against Joan, **inciting hatred and distrust toward her.** The aggressor has successfully manipulated the community's perception, and Joan's character is now vilified.

At this stage, no matter how eloquently Joan defends herself, it is futile. The community has lost all trust and respect for her, making them unwilling to believe anything she says. The aggressor has effectively isolated Joan, and her efforts to regain credibility fall on deaf ears, as the community is now consumed by the aggressor's narrative of hate.

Does this sound familiar to you? It should. It's used in politics all the time!

3. The Crisis Phase: Aggression Peaks and Becomes Dangerous (High Risk):

The **Crisis Phase includes Stages 7 through 9,** and is the final stage of the Aggression Continuum, where aggressive behavior has reached its peak and violence or other harmful actions are imminent. At this stage, the aggressor may no longer be capable of rational decision-making, and the risk to others is high. Immediate intervention is required to contain the situation and prevent harm.

Chapter 5

In Stage 7, the aggressor moves from contemplating (ideation) an attack (physical or professional) against their victim (Stage 6) to planning and preparing for attack. These are the action taken just prior to the actual attack. They can include organizing other participants, surveying locations, determining response times and action taken by protectors like security or law enforcement.

Alternatively in Stage 7, we can have someone who is on a path to intimidate their victim into submission, i.e., to control them. Here the aggressor uses coercion as implied or direct threat of violence if they refuse submission.

In Stage 8, The aggressor makes their plans actionable with intent to "shock and awe!" Although they are prepared to give up their lives for this cause, it is their intent to survive, and their behavior will reflect this intention. Plans are executed. The victim dies physically or professionally.

In Stage 9, is the ultimate of Lose/Lose! This aggressor is committed to destroying the enemy with no intention to survive (perpetrator of murder/suicide). This aggressor may choose to harm their victim (potentially their parents) through self-destruction (suicide), or worse yet, they become a perpetrator of murder/suicide.

The Thousand Yard Stare:

It is important to mention that when any human being, regardless of their culture, gender, education, age, sexual orientation, or religion, reaches a point of commitment where they are prepared to give up their life for a cause, their body undergoes a profound transformation. Their **intention** manifests physically, and the body begins to lose its natural animation, as if signaling, "I'm already dead." This look, often referred to in military circles as the **"thousand-yard stare"** or **"dead eyes,"** is not just a shift in facial expression. The entire body reflects this state—losing vitality, becoming robotic, and detached. The Israelis even call this the **"walking dead,"** as it describes a person who has already resigned themselves to their fate.

Recognizing this distinct body language and behavior is imperative for prevention. **First observers**—whether in parking lots, garages, at drop-off points, or bus operators—need to be trained to detect this transformation. By identifying these early signals, we gain a crucial opportunity to intervene, perhaps just moments before that horrific "Moment of Commitment". This small window of time could be the difference between preventing a tragedy or witnessing its devastating aftermath.

Example of the Crisis Phase:

Tom, a student at a high school in Georgia, has been showing signs of escalating aggression for weeks. His teachers noticed his increasing agitation, aggressive language, and hostile interactions with classmates, but no formal system was in place to flag these behaviors. One day, Tom brings a weapon to school with the intent to harm a classmate who he believes has wronged him.

At this point, Tom has entered the **Crisis Phase**, and immediate action is required to protect both Tom and those around him. Unfortunately, because no early intervention occurred, Tom's behavior escalated to the point where violence was imminent. If CAPS had been in place, Tom's early warning signs during the **Trigger** and **Escalation** Phases could have been detected, allowing for intervention long before the situation became dangerous.

Recognizing the Precursor Signs: Early Detection is Key

The key to preventing aggressive behavior from escalating into violence is recognizing the **precursor signs** at each stage of the continuum. In the **Trigger Phase**, aggression is subtle, but these early warning signs are critical for intervention. In the **Escalation Phase**, aggression becomes more overt and easier to detect, but intervention can still prevent the situation from reaching the **Crisis Phase**.

By training **Aggression First Observers** to spot early behaviors and empowering **Certified Aggression Managers** to intervene effectively, CAPS enables schools to identify and address aggression before it leads to harm. Each stage offers a window for intervention, and the earlier the intervention, the more likely it is to prevent violence or other serious outcomes.

Case Study: Early Intervention in Action

At a middle school in Illinois, the CAPS system flagged a student, Emily, who had been exhibiting signs of emotional distress. Emily's teachers had noticed her withdrawal from social activities, increased irritability, and declining academic performance—classic signs of the **Trigger Phase**. The school's **Certified Aggression Manager** met with Emily and discovered that she was dealing with bullying at home from a sibling.

By addressing Emily's emotional distress early on, the CAM helped her regain control of her emotions and provided her with the support she needed to cope. As a result, Emily's behavior improved, and she was able to re-engage with her peers in a positive way. Without this early intervention, Emily's frustration could have escalated into more serious aggressive behavior.

The Meter of Emerging Aggression (MEA):

The Meter of Emerging Aggression is CAPS's **Central Analysis Tool** found in every CAPS Mobile App, designed to not only detect when an individual is exhibiting aggressive behavior but also to identify the specific **Stage or Level** of aggression they are in. By pinpointing where an individual falls on the aggression continuum, this tool empowers its user to respond with the appropriate skills that will maximize the effectiveness of their de-escalation or redirection efforts. The precision of this tool ensures that interventions are timely and tailored to the severity of the aggression, enhancing the likelihood of diffusing and/or redirecting the situation successfully.

The Conversion of the Primal & Cognitive Aggression Continua to the Meter of Emerging Aggression:

We have distilled the Primal and Cognitive Aggression Continua into seven actionable categories: **Behavior, Communication, Interaction, Demeanor, Tactical Movement, and Other Concerning Factors**. These categories allow for a more comprehensive understanding of aggression, and in this book, we will focus on the Behavior category.

Aggression First Observers (AFO) witnesses aggressive behavior, they go into CAPS Mobile App and select from each appropriate category the corresponding description that matches their observations (Behavior, Communication, Interaction, Demeanor, Tactical Movement, and Other Concerning Factors). By doing so they are selecting aggressive precursors that are scientifically reliable and that do you violate privacy regulations. In the CAPS Mobile App that will be able to report other elements such as logistics to the event; however, none of these elements will be used to determine the level of aggression or the corresponding risk. In this way we avoid any change of violating HIPAA, FERPA, or the Civil Rights Act of 1964.

For those seeking a more detailed understanding, the full Meter of Emerging Aggression, with in-depth descriptions for each category, is available through the CAPS Mobile App. Additionally, you can access complete instructional material through our Aggression First Observers' Course and the Certified Aggression Managers' Course for a comprehensive training and mastery in identifying and addressing aggression.

Interested in Mastering Aggression Prevention?

If you're looking to gain comprehensive training in identifying and preventing aggression, consider enrolling in our **Aggression First Observers' Online Course** and **Certified Aggression Managers' Online Course**. These courses offer the knowledge and tools for early identification and prevention of aggression.

To get started, simply contact us:

- **Phone**: (407) 718-5637
- **Email**: info@AggressionManagement.com

Upon completion of the Certified Aggression Managers' Course, you'll receive a **Certificate of Completion** from the Center for Aggression Management, Inc.

Conclusion: Why Understanding the Aggression Continuum Matters

Recognizing and responding to aggression at every stage of the continuum is essential for maintaining a safe and supportive school environment. The earlier signs of aggression are identified, the more opportunities schools

Chapter 5

have to intervene and redirect students toward healthier, more productive, assertive behaviors. The **Aggression Continuum and its Meter of Emerging Aggression** provides a roadmap for understanding how aggression develops and progresses, empowering schools to take proactive steps to prevent violence and other harmful outcomes.

In the next chapter, we'll explore how CAPS not only prevents violence but also addresses and prevents issues like **sexual harassment**, **bullying**, **conflict**, and **discrimination** by identifying their precursor signs within the Aggression Continuum.

Chapter 6

TRUST: THE FOUNDATION OF PREVENTION AND PERSUASION

Introduction: The Role of Trust in Aggression Prevention

At the heart of every successful interaction lies one critical element: **trust**. Trust is the cornerstone of any relationship, whether personal or professional, and it plays an especially vital role when we are trying to steer someone away from a destructive, aggressive path toward a more positive and constructive one. In the world of Aggression Management, trust allows us to engage individuals in a way that opens them up to new possibilities, including adopting more productive behaviors.

The Critical Aggression Prevention System (CAPS) identifies and measures aggressive behaviors, but the process of redirecting those behaviors requires a human touch: the establishment of trust. Without it, even the best insights into aggression will fail to make a meaningful impact. But when trust is engendered, the potential for persuasion and positive change is unlocked.

Humans, by nature, tend to do what they believe is in their best interest. This fundamental psychological principle guides their behavior. To persuade someone to change course, they must first believe that what you are asking them to do is in their best interest, and they will only believe that if they trust you. Therefore, in the context of CAPS, trust isn't just a helpful factor—it's essential.

The Power of Trust in Human Behavior

Trust creates a connection between individuals that transcends data and logic. In the process of preventing aggression, trust serves as a bridge, allowing one person to guide another to safety. When someone trusts you fully, they will follow your lead—whether you are redirecting them from aggressive behavior, guiding them through conflict resolution, or encouraging more constructive problem-solving.

The absence of trust, however, leads to defensiveness, resistance, and sometimes, a deepening of the very aggression we aim to prevent. Distrust makes people cling more tightly to their destructive behaviors, as they perceive anyone trying to change their course as a threat. This is why trust must be established early on in any intervention strategy within CAPS.

While trust is the foundation of behavior change, surprisingly few systems measure it. There are countless metrics to evaluate performance, productivity, and even teamwork, but trust is largely intangible, often assumed rather than measured. CAPS is transformative in that it helps identify behaviors associated with distrust and provides strategies to redirect them toward trustful behaviors, making it a measurable and actionable factor in violence prevention.

Trust as a Measure of Success

Interestingly, trust is a key driver behind some of the most important aspects of performance, whether in schools, workplaces, or other organizational settings. By fostering trust, we enhance teamwork, leadership, loyalty, productivity, and even profitability in profit-based organizations or institutions. The same can be said for schools, where a climate of trust between students, teachers, and administrators can drastically improve behavior, morale, and academic success.

CAPS allows us to indirectly measure trust by identifying distrustful behaviors. Through the use of scientific methods, CAPS pinpoints moments where aggressive or defensive behaviors are emerging—often a signal of distrust. By focusing on these early warning signs, CAPS provides the opportunity to intervene and redirect aggression toward more cooperative, trustful behaviors. In doing so, we can not only prevent violence but foster environments where trust becomes the norm, not the exception.

Engendering Trust Through Commonality

So how do we engender trust? The answer lies in one of the most fundamental human instincts: the need for connection. Trust is built when people feel a sense of commonality with each other, whether it's through shared experiences, backgrounds, or values. To build trust, we must find and emphasize what we have in common with the individual in question.

In the context of CAPS, one of the most effective strategies for building trust is simply finding common ground. When someone is becoming aggressive—whether in a school, workplace, or other setting—it can often be traced back to a breakdown of trust. The individual no longer feels connected to those around them, leading them to act out frustration, anger, or even tears.

To counter this, we can use a technique I call the **"walk and talk"** strategy. For instance, if you are an Assistant Principal dealing with a student who is showing signs of aggression, and your words are not calming them down, you can say, "Let's go for a walk." The simple act of leaving the room where the tension resides, gives both you and the student a fresh start. You are symbolically leaving the problem behind for a moment.

As you walk, you engage the student in conversation about things you have in common: "Didn't you grow up in this community?" "Didn't we both attend the same school?" "I remember Ms. Smith—was she your teacher too?" Through these questions, you're no longer seen as just an authority figure; you become a person with shared experiences. This helps build rapport, and rapport is the first step toward trust.

By the time you return to the office to discuss the original issue, the dynamic has shifted. Trust has begun to replace the initial tension, making the student far more likely to open up and work with you rather than against you. They now see you not just as someone telling them what to do, but as someone who understands and shares a part of their world.

This strategy works across various settings, including workplaces and even social situations where conflict arises. Commonality fosters a sense of understanding, and understanding creates the foundation upon which trust is built.

Practical Applications of Trust in CAPS

Trust, once established, allows us to guide individuals out of aggression and into cooperation. Whether dealing with a student, employee, or someone in a highly charged situation, the principles of CAPS can be applied to identify aggressive or distrustful behavior early and redirect it toward trustful interactions.

Consider the workplace scenario where an employee begins acting out due to stress or feelings of alienation. Using the CAPS framework, you would first recognize the early signs of aggression, such as raised voices, negative body language, or a decline in cooperation. Rather than confronting the employee head-on, which may exacerbate their aggression, you instead focus on building rapport—perhaps by finding shared experiences or acknowledging their stress. Through this process, trust is established, allowing you to de-escalate the situation and guide the employee toward a more constructive state of mind.

Trust: The Ultimate Performance Multiplier

When we talk about trust, we're not just discussing an abstract concept. Trust is a performance multiplier. It enhances every key element of organizational success: teamwork, leadership, productivity, and loyalty. Schools that foster trust between students and teachers see reduced behavioral problems and improved academic performance. Workplaces that emphasize trust see higher levels of collaboration, innovation, and employee retention.

For organizations driven by profit, trust also directly impacts the bottom line. Employees who trust their leaders are more engaged, productive, and loyal, leading to improved profitability. The same principle applies to schools where trust creates an environment conducive to learning, development, and higher achievement scores.

Building Trust with Aggressors: CAPS in Action

The key to CAPS is that it doesn't just stop at identifying aggressive behaviors—it goes further by providing a pathway to turn those behaviors around. By recognizing distrustful actions and redirecting them toward trust, CAPS allows you to prevent not just violence but also bullying in our schools, sexual harassment, abuse, discrimination, and assaultive behavior before it happens. Trust is not only built through empathy and connection but also through consistency and reliability—core tenets of CAPS.

Trust-building strategies, such as finding commonalities and developing rapport, are integral to the CAPS system. They serve as the glue that holds together the scientific approach of CAPS and its practical, human applications. When trust is fostered, the probability of preventing violence and aggression rises exponentially.

Conclusion

In the end, trust is not a nice-to-have—it is a must-have in the realm of aggression prevention. Without trust, even the best systems will struggle to make an impact. But with trust, CAPS becomes a powerful tool, transforming not just behaviors but environments. Through trust, we prevent aggression, foster cooperation, and create safer, more productive schools and workplaces. And it is through trust that CAPS delivers its most profound and lasting results.

This page intentionally left blank

Chapter 7

PREVENTING SEXUAL HARASSMENT, BULLYING, AND DISCRIMINATION BEFORE THEY START

In schools, the early detection of aggression is critical—not only for preventing violence but also for addressing behaviors like **sexual harassment, bullying, conflict,** and **discrimination**. These harmful behaviors often begin subtly, with actions that may seem inconsequential or difficult to detect at first. However, through the **Critical Aggression Prevention System (CAPS)**, schools can identify the **precursors** to these behaviors in their early stages, preventing them from escalating into more severe incidents.

This chapter focuses on how **CAPS** leverages the **Aggression Continuum** to prevent sexual harassment, bullying, conflict, and discrimination. By recognizing early warning signs, schools can intervene before these behaviors take root, creating a safer, more inclusive environment for all students.

Identifying the Early Precursors to Harmful Behaviors

Sexual harassment, bullying, conflict, and discrimination don't appear suddenly—they follow a pattern that begins with **subtle, often covert behaviors**. These early precursor-signs of aggression may not always be recognized for what they are, which is why it's crucial for school personnel to be trained in spotting **precursor behaviors**.

The Aggression Continuum and Precursors

The **Aggression Continuum** highlights that aggression builds over time, starting with **Trigger Phase** behaviors and someone who is not coping with these triggers, if left unchecked, can escalate into more overt forms of harm. The same is true for harassment, bullying, conflict, and discrimination. Often, these behaviors are masked by passive-aggressive remarks, social exclusion, or other seemingly minor actions, but they are early indicators that a student is moving along the aggression continuum toward more serious harm.

Common Precursors to Harassment, Bullying, and Discrimination:

- **Passive-Aggressive Behavior**: Comments or actions intended to harm others indirectly, such as making subtle jokes or remarks that undermine or belittle.

- **Social Exclusion**: Deliberately exclude someone from social groups or activities as a way of isolating them.

- **Rumor-Spreading**: Sharing false or damaging information about others in an attempt to harm their reputation.

- **Microaggressions**: Subtle, indirect expressions of bias or prejudice, which may not be immediately recognizable as harassment or discrimination but are harmful over time.

These behaviors are often dismissed or ignored because they seem insignificant in isolation. However, in many cases, they are the **first signs** of a more serious pattern of harassment, bullying, or discrimination that will escalate if not addressed.

When people ask if Aggression Management is simply another form of "Anger Management," I respond unequivocally: "Absolutely not!" I explain that in my view, "if you can't measure it, you can't manage it." Anger is a subjective emotion; you and I can experience and express anger in entirely different ways, making it difficult to measure—and, as a result, difficult to manage effectively.

Aggression, on the other hand, is observable and measurable with scientific reliability. This makes it not only easier to manage in others but also in ourselves. In my opinion, it's fine to feel anger—what matters is how we respond to it. It is never okay to let that anger turn into aggression.

How CAPS Prevents These Behaviors Before They Escalate

The power of **CAPS** lies in its ability to detect these **early precursor signs** and intervene before they escalate into an incident. By identifying harmful behaviors early in the **Trigger Phase** or **Escalation Phase**, schools can prevent more serious incidents from occurring. CAPS enables schools to move from a reactive stance—where bullying, sexual harassment, abuse, and discrimination are only addressed after they've caused harm—to a **proactive stance** that stops these behaviors before they occur.

Step 1: Early Detection through Aggression First Observers

Aggression First Observers (AFOs) are trained to recognize the subtle behaviors that often precede sexual harassment, bullying, and discrimination. These individuals—whether they are teachers, staff members, or even security personnel—serve as the first line of defense in spotting passive-aggressive behavior, social exclusion, or rumor-spreading.

By logging these early behaviors into the CAPS system, AFOs help create a record of precursor behaviors. This data allows schools to **track patterns** of behavior over time, providing critical insights into whether a student is moving along the aggression continuum toward more serious behaviors.

Step 2: Intervention by Certified Aggression Managers

Once a pattern of aggressive behavior has been identified, **Certified Aggression Managers (CAMs)** step in to intervene. CAMs are equipped to manage both **Primal** and **Cognitive Aggression**, which means they can address both adrenaline-driven and harmful-intent-driven forms of harassment, bullying, and discrimination.

For instance, a trained Critical Aggression Manager (CAM) might recognize that a student's passive-aggressive comments are the early signs of bullying behavior. The CAM would then step in to engage the student, helping them understand the harm their actions are causing, while offering a more constructive way to achieve their underlying goals—whether that's building social status, seeking acceptance, or managing difficult emotions. By discussing the potential negative consequences of continuing down this path, the CAM helps the student realize the risks involved, including damaged relationships or disciplinary action. At the same time, the CAM presents a more positive path forward, demonstrating how making better choices can not only prevent harm but also serve the student's best interests in the long run.

This approach allows the student to see the benefit of change, ultimately encouraging self-reflection and positive behavioral adjustments. Let me know if you need more adjustments! By addressing these behaviors early, CAMs not only prevent the immediate harm but also stop the aggressor from continuing down the path toward more severe behaviors.

Step 3: Continuous Monitoring and Support

CAPS doesn't just stop at one intervention. The system enables continuous **monitoring** of student behavior, ensuring that once an intervention has been made, the student's progress is tracked over time. This ongoing support helps reinforce positive behaviors and prevent a return to harmful actions. It also allows schools to adjust their approach if the initial intervention wasn't entirely successful.

Preventing Sexual Harassment in Schools

Sexual harassment in schools often begins with subtle behaviors—jokes, comments, or gestures that may seem insignificant but create an uncomfortable or hostile environment for the target. Left unchecked, these behaviors can escalate into more overt forms of harassment, including unwanted physical contact or explicit verbal harassment.

Early Precursor Signs of Sexual Harassment:

- Inappropriate jokes or comments about a student's appearance or personal life.
- Unwanted attention or advances, even if disguised as humor or flirtation.
- Objectification of students, often in the form of comments or rumors.

However, harassment doesn't always manifest in obvious ways. More subtle precursor signs may include behavioral changes such as becoming increasingly uncooperative, nonproductive, or detached. The individual may show a growing lack of empathy, create emotional or social distance from peers, and/or engage in deceptive actions to conceal their aggression.

By recognizing these behaviors in their earliest stages, CAPS allows schools to intervene before it becomes an incident of sexual harassment. You have prevented an innocent person becoming a victim and you have prevented an aggressive person becoming a perpetrator of sexual harassment. For example, if an Aggression First Observer (AFO) logs multiple instances of a student making inappropriate comments to a peer, this can be flagged by the CAPS system and addressed by a Critical Aggression Monitor (CAM) before it escalates into an incident of sexual harassment. Everyone wins!

Preventing Bullying Before It Starts

Bullying, like harassment, often begins with small, seemingly insignificant actions that can spiral into more harmful behavior. It may start with exclusion from social activities, passive-aggressive remarks, or online rumors. These actions are often the **early stages** of **Cognitive Aggression**, where the aggressor is acting deliberately to harm their target's social standing or emotional well-being.

Early precursor-signs of Bullying:

- **Social exclusion**: Deliberately leaving someone out of social groups, conversations, or activities.
- **Gossip and rumors**: Spreading false or harmful information about a peer.
- **Passive-aggressive remarks**: Making subtle comments intended to undermine or belittle another student.

However, bullying doesn't always manifest in obvious ways. More subtle precursor signs may include behavioral changes such as becoming increasingly uncooperative, nonproductive, or detached. The individual may show a growing lack of empathy, create emotional or social distance from peers, and engage in deceptive actions to conceal their aggression.

By recognizing these behaviors in their earliest stages, CAPS allows schools to intervene before it becomes an incident of bullying. You have prevented an innocent person becoming a victim and you have prevented an aggressive person becoming a perpetrator of bullying. For example, if an Aggression First Observer (AFO) logs multiple instances of a student making inappropriate comments to a peer, this can be flagged by the CAPS system and addressed by a Critical Aggression Monitor (CAM) before it escalates into an incident of bullying. Everyone wins!

Chapter 7

Preventing Discrimination in Schools

Discrimination, whether based on race, gender, sexual orientation, religion, or other factors, often manifests in **microaggressions**—small, often unintentional acts of bias or prejudice. These microaggressions can accumulate over time, creating a hostile or unwelcoming environment for the targeted student. Left unchecked, microaggressions can escalate into more overt forms of discrimination, exclusion, or harassment.

Early precursor-signs of Discrimination:

- **Microaggressions**: Small, indirect expressions of bias, such as dismissive comments or stereotypical assumptions about a student's background.

- **Exclusion or isolation**: Deliberately exclude a student from activities or social groups based on their identity.

- **Stereotyping**: Making assumptions about a student's abilities, interests, or behavior based on their race, gender, or other characteristics.

However, discrimination doesn't always manifest in obvious ways. More subtle precursor signs may include behavioral changes such as becoming increasingly uncooperative, nonproductive, or detached. The individual may show a growing lack of empathy, create emotional or social distance from peers, and engage in deceptive actions to conceal their aggression.

By recognizing these behaviors in their earliest stages, CAPS allows schools to intervene before discrimination becomes more severe. For example, if an Aggression First Observer (AFO) logs multiple instances of a student making inappropriate comments to a peer, this can be flagged by the CAPS system and addressed by a Critical Aggression Manger (CAM) before it escalates into an incident of discrimination.

Real-World Example: Stopping Harassment Before It Escalates

At a high school in New York, a female student, Emily, was repeatedly subjected to **inappropriate jokes and comments** from a group of male students in her class. While the comments were framed as jokes, they made Emily uncomfortable, and over time, the behavior escalated. Fortunately, an AFO noticed the pattern of comments and logged them into the CAPS system. A CAM then intervened, addressing the behavior with the male students and helping them understand the impact of their actions.

Because CAPS detected that Emily is not coping during the **Trigger Phase** and engage prior to Emily reached the 4th Stage of the Cognitive Aggression Continuum where Sexual Harassment begins, the situation was resolved before it escalated into an incident of sexual harassment. Emily was able to return to class feeling supported and safe, and the male students learned to change their behavior before it caused more harm.

Conclusion: The Power of Prevention

Sexual harassment, bullying, and discrimination don't happen overnight. They start small, often with behaviors that are easy to overlook. However, by using **CAPS** to identify the **early precursor signs** of these behaviors, schools can intervene before they escalate into more serious incidents. CAPS empowers schools to take a **preventive** approach, addressing harmful behaviors in their infancy and creating a safer, more supportive environment for all students.

In the next chapter, we'll explore how CAPS helps manage aggression and harmful behaviors during the **Escalation and Crisis Phases**, and how schools can handle high-risk situations effectively.

This page intentionally left blank

Chapter 8

CRISIS PHASE: MANAGING HIGH-RISK AGGRESSION

Aggression follows a predictable path, and while early intervention can often prevent harmful outcomes, there are times when aggression has already reached a more advanced stage. When aggression escalates, or when it peaks in the **Crisis Phase**, schools face the highest risk of violence, serious bullying, or severe harassment. Managing these **high-risk** situations requires precision, insight, and immediate action.

In this chapter, we'll explore how **Critical Aggression Prevention System (CAPS)** helps schools handle aggression once it enters the **Crisis Phases**. We will also discuss how **Certified Aggression Managers (CAMs)** can effectively intervene to de-escalate even the most critical situations.

The Crisis Phase: Recognizing Moderate-Risk Behaviors (Stages 7-9):

The **Crisis Phase** represents (Stages 7-9) a critical turning point in the Aggression Continuum. This is where aggressive personalities, initial frustration, stress, or strategic intent intensify, resulting in behaviors that are increasingly aggressive and difficult to manage. While some of these behaviors may still appear as controlled or calculated (Cognitive Aggression), others may involve emotional outbursts and impulsive actions (Primal Aggression).

Once aggression moves into the Crisis Phase, the risk of harm to others—whether physical, emotional, or psychological—dramatically increases. However, intervention is still possible, and managing aggression during this phase can prevent it from advancing into a full-blown crisis.

Chapter 8

Signs of the Crisis Phase:

- **Verbal Aggression**: The individual begins using hostile or threatening language, often aimed at a specific target. Ultimately this aggressor become difficult to understand because as a Primal Aggression they are losing control to a point where they are losing their ability to communicate and they may begin actually exhibiting animalist behavior, such as growly.

- **Heightened Tension**: The aggressor displays physical signs of stress, such as clenching fists, pacing, or making abrupt movements. This person as a Primal Aggressor becomes the "Red faced ready to explode person."

- **Increased Preparation for and Executing Their Attack** : Cognitive aggressors become more deliberate and targeted in their behavior, attempting to undermine, isolate, or control others through covert means. Ultimately this aggressors are planning or preparing for an attack, they then become operational either with the intent to survive or give up their lives for their cause.

- **Polarizing Behavior**: The aggressor now sees all situations in black-and-white terms, with no room for compromise or discussion. The middle ground has disappeared, and their interactions are creating a plan and executing that plan.

Example of the Crisis Phase:

In a middle school in Texas, a student named Kevin began showing signs of verbal aggression toward a classmate, Jason. Initially, Kevin's behavior started with minor irritability, but as time passed, he began making openly hostile comments and spreading rumors about Jason. Kevin's physical tension was also evident—he clenched his fists during class discussions and avoided eye contact.

Stage 7 aggressive behavior doesn't always manifest in obvious ways. More subtle precursor signs may include **covert planning of an attack**. This could involve Kevin silently forming plans to harm Jason or disrupt the school environment, but without directly acting yet. Kevin might begin to engage in more calculated behavior, either on his own or in collaboration with others, such as gathering tools or materials necessary for his plan, or surveying a potential attack points or circumstances, but doing so without drawing attention to himself.

Stage 8 aggressive behavior involves the aggressor becoming operational, and the attack is imminent. At this stage, Kevin may begin to take concrete, visible steps toward carrying out his plan, such as obtaining weapons, timing the attack, and finalizing details. However, a key aspect of Stage 8 is that Kevin intends to survive the attack. He may have planned an escape route or is considering how to evade capture afterward. Kevin could be openly discussing his plans with others, recruiting help, or practicing specific elements of the attack. His behavior may become more erratic as the time of the attack approaches, but his goal is to survive and continue his actions afterward.

Stage 9 aggressive behavior represents the final preparation and execution of the attack, but with a fundamental difference: Kevin knows he will not survive. At this stage, the aggression escalates to the point where Kevin has accepted that he will either die by "suicide by cop" or take his own life in a murder-suicide scenario. His behavior may now include finalizing notes, videos, or other statements that justify his actions or explain his motivations. By now, Kevin has emotionally committed to dying for his cause, and any hesitation or doubt has been resolved. He typically will exhibit a profound calm, as the certainty of his death has solidified his mindset. The violence is imminent and will be carried out with the knowledge that it will also end his life.

Recognizing these signs, an **Aggression First Observer (AFO)** reported the behavior to the school's **Certified Aggression Manager (CAM)**. I would never say that it's too late, because if there is a muster seed of rationale Kevin can be turned away from his commitment; however, the opportunity have become dire. By catching Kevin's aggression during the **Crisis Phase**, the CAM can prevent this from reaching a crisis point by getting out in front of that horrific "Moment of Commitment" that we have discussed earlier.

Managing the Crisis Phase with CAPS

When a student reaches the Crisis Phase, CAPS equips schools with the tools to handle these potential **high-risk situations** swiftly and effectively. While other systems may focus solely on crisis response after the fact, CAPS emphasizes **early pre-incident precursor-detection and**

intervention. In this way CAPS significantly reduces the number of incidents that reach this critical point. However, when crises do occur, the system remains an invaluable tool for managing them.

Certified Aggression Managers (CAMs) as Part of the Threat Assessment Team

In schools, workplaces, and other environments where safety is paramount, Certified Aggression Managers (CAMs) play a critical role in identifying and mitigating aggressive behavior before it escalates into violence. These individuals, all highly trained in CAPS, are often part of a Threat Assessment Team—a group of professionals dedicated to the prevention of violence through careful analysis and intervention. On school campuses they may also be called a Behavioral Intervention Team (BIT).

The Threat Assessment Team consists of a cross-section of professionals, each bringing unique expertise to the table but united by their comprehensive CAPS training. These teams are specifically designed to monitor, assess, and respond to early indicators of aggression and threats, ensuring that any situation can be managed swiftly and effectively. CAMs within these teams are trained to use pre-incident de-escalation and redirection techniques, allowing them to intervene long before an act of aggression can escalate into violence.

The team includes:

School Resource Officers (SROs): Their familiarity with the student body and their role in maintaining school safety make SROs key members of the Threat Assessment Team. With CAPS training, SROs can handle not only physical security but also the early detection of aggressive behaviors, addressing them before they become a crisis.

Mental Health Counselors: Counselors provide invaluable insight into the emotional and psychological aspects of aggression. As members of the Threat Assessment Team, they apply CAPS techniques to understand and redirect aggressive behaviors, addressing root causes such as stress, trauma, or conflict.

School Safety Officers: These officers ensure the physical security of the school, but with CAPS training, they become proactive participants in identifying and managing aggressive behavior. Their role in the team is crucial for both preventing physical altercations and creating a safe environment.

Administrative Staff: Principals, assistant principals, and other administrators, when trained as CAMs, bring a leadership perspective to the Threat Assessment Team. They are often the first to respond to disciplinary issues, and with CAPS, they shift from reactive discipline to proactive aggression management, fostering a safer and more cooperative school culture.

Each member of the Threat Assessment Team is highly trained in CAPS, which enables them to identify the subtle and overt signs of aggression, perform in-depth threat assessments, and take action before an incident occurs. The diversity of the team ensures that aggression is understood and managed from multiple perspectives—emotional, physical, and environmental—resulting in a comprehensive and effective approach to violence prevention.

Prevention at the Core: Engaging Early to Avoid Stages 7, 8, and 9

One of the core strengths of CAPS is its ability to engage with aggressive behavior early, before it escalates into severe violence. By identifying and intervening at **Stages 3, 4, and 5**, CAPS-trained professionals can prevent individuals from reaching the more dangerous stages of **7, 8, and 9**, where the likelihood of an attack becomes significantly higher.

It is our expectation that through early intervention, we will encounter a rare number of cases that reach Stages 7, 8, and 9. The goal of CAPS is to address aggression at its formative stages, using proven techniques for de-escalation and redirection. By focusing on **early-stage aggression**, we can steer individuals away from a path of escalating violence, ensuring that the threat is neutralized long before it reaches a critical point.

Certified Aggression Managers (CAMs), as part of a Threat Assessment Team, are equipped to intervene at these early stages, identifying signs of verbal aggression, irritability, or covert hostility (Stages 3 through 5). By the time an individual might begin planning a physical attack (Stage 7), or worse, committing to an act with the intent of not surviving (Stage 9), the intervention has already taken place, and the individual has been redirected toward more constructive, trust-based paths.

This proactive approach is what sets CAPS apart. Instead of waiting until an individual reaches the more dangerous phases, CAPS empowers teams to intervene early, effectively preventing these aggressive behaviors from developing into something far more destructive. The result is a safer environment where serious threats rarely, if ever, materialize into real danger.

Conclusion: Managing High-Risk Aggression with Confidence

The **Crisis Phases** represent the most critical points on the Aggression Continuum, where the risk of harm to students and staff is highest. However, with the right tools and training, schools can manage even these high-risk situations effectively. **Certified Aggression Managers** are trained to intervene with precision, using de-escalation techniques to prevent aggression from spiraling out of control.

While CAPS is invaluable in managing high-risk aggression, its true strength lies in prevention. By catching early precursor-signs of aggression, schools can stop students from ever reaching the Crisis Phase. In the next chapter, we'll delve into the **scientific foundation of CAPS**, exploring how the system achieves prevention with scientific reliability and protects students while adhering to privacy regulations.

Chapter 9

The Science Behind CAPS: Preventing Aggression with Scientific Reliability

The **Critical Aggression Prevention System (CAPS)** is not just another program aimed at managing school violence or aggression. What sets CAPS apart is its **scientific foundation**, which allows it to prevent aggression with a high degree of **reliability**. This chapter explores the research and technology behind CAPS, explaining how the system works to identify early precursor-signs of aggression and intervene effectively, while maintaining compliance with strict privacy regulations like **FERPA**, **HIPAA**, and the **Civil Rights Act of 1964**.

The Scientific Reliability of CAPS

CAPS is built on decades of research into human behavior, aggression, and early intervention strategies. It has been scientifically reliable through rigorous studies, including research conducted at **Eastern Kentucky University**, which confirmed the system's ability to reliably identify aggression in its early stages.

At the core of CAPS is the **Aggression Continuum**, a model that tracks the progression of aggressive behavior from subtle emotional responses to disconnections, to outright violence. This continuum, combined with CAPS' scientifically reliable methods for early detection, allows schools to intervene long before aggression reaches a critical point.

Key Principles Behind CAPS:

- **Primal and Cognitive Aggression Continua**: CAPS distinguishes between **Primal Aggression** (impulsive, emotional aggression) and **Cognitive Aggression** (calculated, intent-driven aggression). This distinction is essential because each form of aggression requires a different approach. CAPS teaches schools how to identify which type of aggression is at play and how to respond accordingly.

- **Sequential Successive Precursors**: CAPS identifies aggression through observable **precursor behaviors**, which occur sequentially as aggression progresses. By detecting these behaviors early, CAPS enables schools to intervene before violence, harassment, bullying, or discrimination occur.

- **Behavior-Based Observation**: CAPS is rooted in **observable behaviors**, not assumptions or personal characteristics. This allows schools to remain compliant with privacy laws while still addressing aggression effectively. CAPS does not require access to personal information, but instead focuses on visible actions and scientifically reliable indicators.

How CAPS Achieves Scientific Reliability

CAPS: A Data-Driven, Real-Time Approach to Aggression Prevention

What sets the **Critical Aggression Prevention System (CAPS)** apart from traditional approaches to violence prevention is its reliance on **data-driven methods**. Schools and organizations using CAPS can trust that aggression is being identified with **scientific reliability**, based on solid, repeatable evidence rather than subjective opinions or guesswork. This ensures that every intervention is grounded in measurable data, providing administrators, school resource officers, and other professionals with confidence in the system's effectiveness.

CAPS functions as a **real-time system**, allowing users to observe and respond to aggression as it unfolds. Aggressive behaviors are not only captured as they occur but also **monitored continuously**, ensuring that any change in behavior—whether a decrease or escalation—is immediately detected. This enables teams to take action quickly, preventing situations from spiraling out of control.

The power of real-time data means that those using CAPS can **see the direct impact** of their interventions. From identifying the initial signs of aggression to implementing a de-escalation strategy, and finally recording the result of the action taken, everything is logged and analyzed. This creates an **ongoing feedback loop** where every incident informs future decisions, and the system is constantly refined and adapted to ensure optimal outcomes.

Further, because CAPS tracks all interactions and behavioral changes, it provides a robust, evidence-based record of each case. This continuous monitoring allows users to follow the trajectory of an individual's behavior over time, ensuring that even subtle shifts in aggression are captured, acted upon, and recorded. This level of precision provides schools with a **comprehensive safety net**, making it possible to address aggressive behavior long before it can escalate into violence.

By employing CAPS, schools can rest assured that they are using a system backed by **scientific reliability**, one that operates in real-time and offers ongoing, data-based monitoring. The result is a safer, more controlled environment where aggression is managed and prevented with proven effectiveness.

Real-Time Data Collection

The CAPS system uses real-time data from **Aggression First Observers (AFOs)** and **Certified Aggression Managers (CAMs)** to track and document behaviors as they occur. This data is logged into the **CAPS Mobile App**, which is used to monitor students and identify patterns of behavior that may indicate rising aggression. By collecting and analyzing data over time, CAPS is able to flag students who are moving along the aggression continuum, allowing schools to act before a situation escalates.

Pattern Recognition and Analysis

One of the most powerful aspects of CAPS is its ability to **recognize patterns** in behavior. For instance, if a student begins showing signs of irritability, social withdrawal, or verbal aggression, CAPS tracks these behaviors and connects them to broader patterns of aggression that may have been missed by teachers or staff.

The system's **dashboard** provides administrators and Certified Aggression Managers with insights into these patterns, allowing them to make informed decisions about interventions. This pattern-based approach increases the system's reliability, ensuring that schools are catching aggression at its earliest stages.

Scientific Validation of Precursors

CAPS has been validated through studies that demonstrate the **reliability** of the precursor behaviors it identifies. These precursors—subtle changes in behavior that signal the beginning stages of aggression—are grounded in decades of psychological research on human behavior and aggression.

For example, signs of **Primal Aggression** such as changes in posture, verbal outbursts, or emotional volatility are scientifically linked to increased aggression risk. Likewise, **Cognitive Aggression**—such as strategic manipulation or passive-aggressive behavior—has been validated as a precursor to more serious conflicts.

Because CAPS is built on these reliable, observable indicators, it can be used consistently across different schools, ensuring that aggression is detected and managed proactively, regardless of the specific individuals involved.

Preventing Aggression Without Violating Privacy Regulations

One of the primary concerns schools face when implementing aggression prevention systems is how to maintain compliance with privacy regulations such as **FERPA** and **HIPAA**. These regulations are essential for protecting the privacy of students and staff, but they can also complicate efforts to identify and address aggression.

CAPS addresses this challenge by focusing solely on **observable aggressive behavior**, not personal characteristics like race, gender, sexual orientation, or other protected categories. This makes CAPS uniquely capable of complying with laws such as the **Civil Rights Act of 1964** while still enabling effective aggression prevention.

FERPA Compliance

FERPA (Family Educational Rights and Privacy Act) regulates the sharing of student information, making it difficult for schools to access or share private data without parental consent. However, CAPS operates within the bounds of FERPA by focusing on aggressive behavior, not personal information. The data logged by CAPS is based on what teachers and staff can see—such as a student's irritability, verbal aggression, or withdrawal from social activities—without delving into private details.

Because CAPS relies on observable behaviors, it allows schools to intervene early without requiring access to sensitive personal information, thus ensuring compliance with FERPA.

CAPS and HIPAA Compliance: Protecting Privacy While Ensuring Safety

One of the most important aspects of CAPS is its HIPAA (Health Insurance Portability and Accountability Act) compliance, which ensures that schools and organizations can prioritize student safety without violating privacy regulations, particularly when it comes to health information. HIPAA protects the privacy of health and mental health records, meaning that access to such information is tightly regulated.

The Critical Aggression Prevention System (CAPS) functions without requiring access to students' medical or psychological records, making it fully compliant with HIPAA. Instead of relying on private health data, CAPS focuses on observable behaviors—patterns that can be identified in day-to-day interactions. For example, if a student begins to show signs of increased anxiety or frustration, a CAPS-trained observer can log these behaviors, track their development, and take appropriate action without ever needing to access or discuss the student's mental health history.

This approach allows schools to remain fully compliant with HIPAA while still addressing potential risks to student and staff safety. CAPS ensures that any interventions are based on behavior patterns visible to everyone involved, not on confidential medical assessments.

Even though CAPS doesn't use mental health assessments, mental health professionals can still play a crucial role on the team. For example, at Eastern Kentucky University (EKU), we had the Director of Mental Health as part of our CAPS team. While she could not and would not discuss mental illness or disorders, she contributed significantly to managing aggressive behaviors by focusing on observable aggression patterns.

Her role was unique: while she was equipped to recognize when an individual's aggression might stem from underlying mental health issues, she was also trained in Aggression Management and could collaborate effectively with the CAPS team. If an aggressor exhibited mental health concerns, she might take the individual down a different path for further support, but the rest of the CAPS team could trust her judgment and expertise in managing aggression within the CAPS framework.

This structure ensures that CAPS not only complies with HIPAA but also leverages the expertise of mental health professionals without compromising privacy or confidentiality. Schools can continue to protect student privacy while effectively preventing violence and managing aggressive behavior with a comprehensive, data-driven, and legally compliant system.

Civil Rights Act Compliance

The **Civil Rights Act of 1964** prohibits discrimination based on race, gender, religion, and other protected categories. CAPS maintains strict compliance with this law by focusing on behavior and avoiding any assumptions or interventions based on personal characteristics. This ensures that CAPS can be applied equally to all students, regardless of their background, and that no student is singled out based on factors unrelated to their behavior.

How CAPS Technology Enables Prevention at Scale

In addition to its scientifically reliable methods, CAPS incorporates technology that allows it to be applied across **large school systems** or **districts** without losing effectiveness. This scalability is made possible by tools like the **CAPS Mobile App**, **CAPS Dashboard**, and **CAPS Online Courses**, which streamline the data collection, analysis, and training processes.

CAPS Mobile App and Dashboard

Although there a **CAPS Mobile Apps for individuals**, The **CAPS Mobile App for schools** enables school staff to log behaviors in real time, ensuring that no precursor sign of aggression is missed. Once logged, this data is analyzed by the system's algorithm, which identifies patterns and provides alerts to Certified Aggression Managers.

The **CAPS Dashboard** aggregates this data into an easy-to-understand format, allowing administrators and CAMs to make informed decisions about which students require intervention and what steps to take next.

CAPS Online Courses

To ensure that school personnel are fully trained in using CAPS, the system offers **online courses** that cover every aspect of the Aggression Continuum, from early warning signs to high-risk behaviors. These courses are designed to be scalable, meaning that they can be rolled out across entire school districts or regions without losing their effectiveness.

Conclusion: A Reliable, Proactive System for Aggression Prevention

CAPS represents a new standard in aggression prevention, offering **scientific reliability** and **scalability** while remaining compliant with privacy regulations. By focusing on observable behaviors and using technology to track and analyze aggression patterns, CAPS allows schools to identify and address aggressive behavior before it spirals out of control.

In the next chapter, we'll explore how CAPS can be tailored to address specific issues in different environments—such as workplaces, healthcare facilities, and universities—and how the system can be adapted to meet the needs of these varied settings.

This page intentionally left blank

Chapter 10
ADAPTING CAPS TO DIFFERENT ENVIRONMENTS: SCHOOLS, WORKPLACES, AND HEALTHCARE

While the **Critical Aggression Prevention System (CAPS)** was initially developed to prevent violence and aggression in schools, its principles and methods can be adapted to various environments where aggression may occur, including **workplaces**, **healthcare facilities**, and **universities**. In each of these settings, CAPS helps create safer, more supportive environments by identifying early precursor-signs of aggression and intervening before situations escalate.

This chapter explores how CAPS can be adapted to meet the unique needs of different environments, focusing on the **commonalities** and **differences** in the challenges these settings face. By understanding how CAPS can be applied in diverse contexts, we can appreciate its flexibility and effectiveness in preventing aggression wherever it arises.

CAPS in Schools: Creating a Safe Learning Environment

In **schools**, CAPS has proven to be an invaluable tool for preventing aggression, bullying, harassment, and violence. Schools are unique environments where students, teachers, staff, and parents all interact daily, making it critical to identify aggression early and address it before it escalates.

Challenges in Schools:

- **High student interaction**: Students engage with each other in classrooms, hallways, playgrounds, and during extracurricular activities. This frequent interaction increases the chances for conflict, making it essential to detect early warning signs of aggression.

- **Bullying and harassment**: Schools are often breeding grounds for bullying and harassment, which can begin with small, seemingly insignificant actions but escalate into serious emotional or physical harm.

- **Developing social and emotional skills**: Students, particularly younger ones, are still learning how to manage their emotions and navigate social situations. This makes early intervention critical in helping them develop healthier ways to handle conflict.

How CAPS Works in Schools:

In schools, CAPS helps by training **Aggression First Observers (AFOs)** and **Certified Aggression Managers (CAMs)** to recognize the **precursor signs** of aggression. Through the use of the **CAPS Mobile App**, teachers and staff can log behaviors such as social withdrawal, irritability, or verbal outbursts. This data is then analyzed by the **CAPS Dashboard**, which helps school administrators understand patterns of behavior and intervene early.

For example, a high school teacher might notice a student becoming increasingly isolated and hostile toward classmates. The teacher logs these behaviors, prompting a CAM to assess the situation. By intervening early, the CAM can work with the student to de-escalate the aggression before it escalates into bullying or violence.

CAPS in the Workplace: Preventing Conflict and Enhancing Productivity

Aggression is not limited to schools. **Workplaces** are also environments where conflicts can arise, leading to reduced productivity, lower morale, and even potential violence. CAPS can be adapted to help businesses create safer, more productive work environments by identifying early precursor-signs of workplace aggression, harassment, and discrimination.

Challenges in Workplaces:

- **Team dynamics**: In professional settings, employees are expected to work together, often in high-pressure situations. This can lead to stress, frustration, and conflict, particularly if communication breaks down.

- **Harassment and discrimination**: Workplaces are also at risk for incidents of harassment and discrimination, which often start subtly with precursors, but can escalate into more serious problems if not addressed early.

- **Overcoming Fear of Retaliation with CAPS:** In many workplaces, employees may be hesitant to report aggressive behavior due to a fear of retaliation or the worry that they will be viewed as disruptive. This hesitation can allow aggression to go unchecked, increasing the risk of escalation. Traditional methods of addressing aggression often rely on punitive measures, which can exacerbate this fear and lead to a culture of silence.

  However, CAPS is different. It is not punitive but rather rehabilitative, focusing on early identification and intervention without punishment or retaliation because no incident occurs. CAPS works by addressing aggression before it reaches a critical incident, using a system of support and redirection that encourages positive behavioral changes. By offering a solution that does not evoke the fear of punishment, CAPS helps foster a safer and more transparent workplace where individuals feel comfortable reporting aggressive behaviors, knowing the goal is prevention and rehabilitation rather than punishment.

How CAPS Works in Workplaces:

In a workplace environment, **Aggression First Observers** may include supervisors, HR personnel, or employees themselves. They are trained to recognize behaviors like passive-aggressive comments, social exclusion, or strategic undermining. Using the **CAPS Mobile App**, these observers can log incidents in real time, providing CAPS trained HR or management with a clear picture of patterns developing within teams or departments.

For example, if an employee starts to withdraw from team meetings and is frequently making sarcastic or passive-aggressive remarks toward colleagues, an AFO might log these behaviors. A **Certified Aggression Manager** can then step in to assess the situation, offering support and de-escalation/redirection strategies to resolve the conflict before it affects productivity or escalates into harassment or bullying.

CAPS for Workplace Compliance:

Workplaces are subject to laws and regulations regarding employee safety, such as **OSHA** standards and anti-harassment policies. While current programs wait until someone is accused of harassment and apply some form of punitive measures against the accused, CAPS not only helps prevent incidents of workplace violence or harassment but also ensures compliance with these regulations by tracking and addressing aggressive behavior in a timely manner, and without violating privacy regulations.

Aggression Management in Healthcare: Addressing Unique Challenges with CAPS

Healthcare facilities, such as hospitals, clinics, and care facilities, present unique challenges when it comes to managing aggression. These environments are often high-stress, with patients, families, and healthcare providers under immense pressure. This stress can sometimes manifest as aggressive behavior, not only from patients but also from staff who are dealing with the emotional and physical demands of their work.

According to the Occupational Safety and Health Administration (OSHA), hospitals and healthcare facilities experience more non-fatal assaults than any other industry. This is a growing concern, especially as healthcare workers face an increasing risk of both verbal and physical aggression. In fact, a recent survey by the American Nurses Association revealed that one-third of all nurses are considering leaving the profession due to the constant threat of assaultive behavior.

This highlights the urgent need for a system that can detect and manage aggression before it escalates. The Critical Aggression Prevention System (CAPS) provides a comprehensive solution. CAPS identifies the early precursor signs of aggression in healthcare settings, allowing trained professionals to intervene before situations spiral out of control. By managing aggression at its early stages, CAPS helps maintain a safer environment for both patients and staff, reducing the risk of assaults and improving the overall well-being of healthcare professionals.

Challenges in Healthcare Settings:

- **Patient and family stress**: Patients and their families are often dealing with fear, uncertainty, and frustration, which can lead to aggressive outbursts or conflicts with healthcare staff.

- **Workplace violence**: According to **OSHA**, healthcare workers are more likely to experience **non-fatal workplace violence** than workers in any other industry. Aggression in healthcare can range from verbal abuse to physical assaults on staff.

- **Burnout and stress among healthcare workers**: Healthcare professionals are often overworked and stressed, which can lead to internal conflicts among staff or result in staff members themselves becoming aggressive toward patients or colleagues.

How CAPS Works in Healthcare:

In healthcare environments, **Aggression First Observers** might include nurses, security staff, and other front-line workers. These individuals are trained to recognize **early precursor-signs of aggression** in patients, families, or even colleagues. For instance, a nurse who notices a patient becoming increasingly agitated might log this behavior into the CAPS system. This allows **Certified Aggression Managers** to intervene before the patient's aggression escalates to physical violence.

Additionally, CAPS can help healthcare administrators track patterns of aggressive behavior across their facilities. For example, if a specific department or unit is experiencing high levels of aggression from patients or staff, the CAPS system can provide insights into the underlying causes, allowing administrators to implement targeted interventions to reduce stress and prevent further incidents.

Real-World Example: Managing Aggression in a Hospital

At a major healthcare facility, CAPS was implemented to address the growing concern of patient aggression toward nursing staff. One day, a patient in the ER began showing signs of escalating frustration after waiting for several hours to be seen. A **Certified Aggression Manager** was alerted after the patient's behavior was logged by a nurse using the **CAPS Mobile App**. The CAM intervened by addressing the patient's concerns, offering reassurance, and managing the situation before the patient became verbally or physically abusive toward staff.

This early intervention not only protected the healthcare workers but also prevented a potentially dangerous situation from escalating further.

Adapting CAPS to Other Environments: Universities, Retail, and Public Spaces

Beyond schools, workplaces, and healthcare, CAPS can be adapted to various other environments where aggression might arise. **Universities**, for instance, face challenges with student interactions, faculty-student relationships, and the complexities of campus life. **Retail environments** often involve conflicts between customers and staff, especially in high-stress situations like sales or shortages of goods. **Public spaces** such as transit systems or government offices are also prone to aggressive incidents.

In each of these environments, the core principles of CAPS remain the same:

- **Identify early precursor-signs of aggression** before they escalate.
- **Use data-driven tools** to track patterns of behavior.
- **Implement targeted interventions** to de-escalate conflicts and prevent harm.

CAPS' flexibility allows it to be customized to fit the specific needs and dynamics of any setting, making it a powerful tool for aggression prevention across industries.

Conclusion: CAPS as a Universal Solution

The versatility of CAPS lies in its ability to adapt to various environments, from schools to workplaces to healthcare facilities. By providing a scientifically reliable system for identifying and managing aggression, CAPS empowers organizations of all types to create safer, more supportive environments.

As we continue to explore the broader applications of CAPS, the next chapter will delve into how CAPS can support **ongoing training** and **professional development** for staff, ensuring that everyone within an organization is equipped to recognize and respond to aggression effectively.

This page intentionally left blank

Chapter 11
ONGOING TRAINING AND PROFESSIONAL DEVELOPMENT WITH CAPS

The effectiveness of the **Critical Aggression Prevention System (CAPS)** lies not only in its ability to identify and manage aggression but also in its emphasis on **ongoing training** and **professional development**. For CAPS to be successful, it's essential that school personnel, workplace staff, healthcare professionals, and others involved in aggression management are fully equipped to recognize early precursor-signs of aggression, intervene effectively, and de-escalate high-risk situations.

This chapter focuses on how CAPS provides comprehensive, scalable training programs for **Aggression First Observers (AFOs)** and **Certified Aggression Managers (CAMs)**, ensuring that individuals at all levels are prepared to take action when aggression begins to manifest.

The Role of Training in CAPS Success

CAPS is designed to be adaptable and scalable, but its success hinges on the **skills and knowledge** of those implementing the system. Training is a core component of the CAPS program, ensuring that participants—from teachers to healthcare workers to corporate managers—are fully capable of recognizing and responding to aggression.

Training for Aggression First Observers (AFOs)

Aggression First Observers (AFOs) are the first line of defense in identifying aggression before it escalates. The training for AFOs is focused on teaching individuals how to:

- **Recognize early precursor-signs of aggression** in both Primal and Cognitive forms.

- **Log observable behaviors** using the **CAPS Mobile App**.

- **Understand the Aggression Continuum** and recognize where an individual's behavior falls along the spectrum.

- **Report behaviors** to **Certified Aggression Managers (CAMs)** for further intervention.

The goal of AFO training is to create a **proactive system** where aggression can be identified early and reported before it escalates into more dangerous or harmful behavior. AFOs are trained to be vigilant in observing student behavior, employee interactions, or patient conduct, depending on the environment where CAPS is applied.

Example of AFO Training in Action: In a middle school, a teacher trained as an AFO noticed a student, Mark, showing signs of **Primal Aggression**—he had become irritable, withdrawn, and was starting to lash out at classmates over minor incidents. The teacher logged Mark's behaviors into the CAPS system and notified the school's CAM. Early intervention helped Mark address his frustrations and prevented the situation from escalating into physical conflict.

Training for Certified Aggression Managers (CAMs)

Certified Aggression Managers (CAMs) receive more advanced training, equipping them with the skills to:

- **Assess the underlying intent** behind aggressive behavior, distinguishing between Primal and Cognitive Aggression.

- **Use de-escalation techniques** to manage aggression in real time, whether it's an emotional outburst or a calculated act of manipulation.

- **Redirect aggression** by guiding individuals toward more constructive behaviors that align with their goals but do not harm others.

- **Monitor behavior patterns** using the **CAPS Dashboard**, identifying trends and determining the best course of action for intervention.

CAMs are taught how to not only diffuse aggression but also **redirect** it toward a positive outcome. This requires a deep understanding of human behavior, communication techniques, and the ability to assess what motivates an aggressor.

Certified Aggression Managers: Beyond Diffusion to Redirection

Let's start with the following premise: **humans tend to do what they perceive is in their best interest**. Certified Aggression Managers are trained not just to de-escalate aggressive situations but to **convince the aggressor that their current path is not in their best interest**. By presenting an alternative (redirecting), more constructive path, CAMs help shift the aggressor's focus toward a positive resolution.

For instance, a CAM might work with a student who is engaging in **Cognitive Aggression**—subtly undermining a classmate through rumor-spreading or manipulation. Instead of simply telling the student to stop, the CAM will engage with the student's underlying motives, helping them see that their behavior, while effective in the short term, will have negative consequences. By offering an alternative path—such as improving communication skills or focusing on collaboration—the CAM redirects the student toward a more constructive approach.

This strategy is based on **persuasion and empowerment**. When an aggressor chooses to follow a more positive path because they see it as **beneficial to their interests**, they are much less likely to return to aggressive behavior in the future. This proactive, prevention-based approach is a key differentiator for CAPS and one that sets it apart from traditional conflict resolution methods.

Ongoing Professional Development: Keeping Skills Sharp

The nature of aggression is constantly evolving, and the contexts in which it occurs—whether in schools, workplaces, or healthcare facilities—are dynamic. As a result, ongoing professional development is essential to keep AFOs and CAMs well-prepared to handle new and emerging challenges.

CAPS Online Courses

CAPS will offer **online courses** for continuing education, ensuring that school staff, employees, and healthcare professionals can refresh their knowledge and stay up-to-date on the latest strategies for managing aggression. These courses cover:

- **Advanced de-escalation techniques**: How to manage aggression in more complex or high-risk scenarios.
- **Behavioral pattern recognition**: How to spot subtler, evolving signs of aggression that may not have been covered in initial training.
- **Case studies and real-world examples**: Learning from actual scenarios where aggression was managed successfully using CAPS principles.

These courses are **scalable** and **accessible**, allowing organizations to provide ongoing training to their staff without the need for in-person sessions. This ensures that everyone involved in aggression management remains confident and prepared.

Workshops and In-Person Training

In addition to online courses, CAPS also offers **workshops** and **in-person training sessions** for organizations that prefer a more hands-on approach. These sessions are particularly valuable in high-stress environments, such as healthcare facilities or large corporations, where face-to-face interaction allows for deeper exploration of aggression management techniques.

Example of Ongoing Training in Healthcare: At a large hospital system, nurses and security personnel undergo **regular training sessions** to refresh their skills in managing patient aggression. These workshops, provided through CAPS, include role-playing exercises and simulated high-stress scenarios, allowing participants to practice de-escalation and redirection techniques in a controlled environment. This ongoing professional development helps staff remain calm and effective even when confronted with aggressive patients or family members.

The Benefits of Continuous Training and Development

Investing in continuous training for AFOs and CAMs ensures that organizations are always ready to respond to aggression. The benefits include:

- **Increased confidence**: Staff feel more prepared to handle aggressive situations, which leads to more successful interventions and greater overall safety.

- **Consistency in response**: Ongoing training ensures that all personnel are using the same techniques and strategies, creating a cohesive approach to aggression management.

- **Adaptability**: As new types of aggression emerge (e.g., online bullying or digital harassment), CAPS training evolves to meet these challenges, keeping AFOs and CAMs ahead of the curve.

Building a Culture of Prevention

By incorporating regular training and professional development into their aggression management strategies, schools, workplaces, and healthcare facilities can build a culture of **prevention** rather than reaction. This culture shift leads to environments where aggression is identified early, addressed swiftly, and resolved in a way that benefits everyone involved.

For CAPS to be fully effective, it must be seen not as a one-time program but as an ongoing commitment to the safety and well-being of everyone in the organization. With continuous training, schools can ensure that staff are always prepared to identify and manage aggression, creating safer, more supportive environments for students and employees alike.

Conclusion: Ensuring Long-Term Success with CAPS

The success of CAPS depends not only on its scientifically reliable methods and advanced technology but also on the **training** and **professional development** of those using it. By investing in the skills of Aggression First Observers and Certified Aggression Managers,

Chapter 11

organizations ensure that they are always ready to prevent aggression before it escalates.

In the next chapter, we'll explore how CAPS can be integrated into broader **organizational safety strategies**, helping schools, businesses, and healthcare systems take a holistic approach to preventing violence and aggression.

Chapter 12
Integrating CAPS into Broader Organizational Safety Strategies

The **Critical Aggression Prevention System (CAPS)** is more than just a tool for managing aggression—it is a cornerstone of a broader strategy for creating safer, more productive environments in schools, workplaces, healthcare facilities, and beyond. By integrating CAPS into an organization's overall **safety framework**, leaders can build comprehensive systems that not only prevent aggression but also enhance team performance, communication, and morale.

In this chapter, we'll explore how CAPS fits into **broader organizational safety strategies** and how its **layered approach** to aggression prevention strengthens the overall safety, well-being, and productivity of an organization. We will also revisit the concepts from the old Chapter 4—particularly the advanced skills of **Certified Aggression Managers (CAMs)** in de-escalating situations and redirecting aggression—and discuss how these skills play a critical role in organizational safety.

The Importance of a Layered Approach to Safety

In any environment—whether a school, corporate office, or healthcare facility—safety must be approached from multiple angles. While physical security measures such as cameras, locked doors, and emergency protocols are critical, they address only the symptoms of an unsafe environment, not the root causes.

CAPS brings a **behavioral dimension** to safety, focusing on identifying and preventing aggression before it manifests as violence or disruption. By integrating CAPS with physical and procedural safety measures, organizations can create a **layered** safety approach that is proactive rather than reactive.

How CAPS Fits into Broader Safety Systems:

- **Behavioral Detection and Prevention**: CAPS focuses on **early detection** of aggressive behaviors and their precursors, allowing organizations to intervene before situations escalate. This is a critical first line of defense, complementing physical safety measures.

- **Real-Time Intervention**: By training **Aggression First Observers (AFOs)** and **Certified Aggression Managers (CAMs)**, CAPS ensures that real-time intervention is possible whenever aggression begins to manifest. This complements other real-time safety measures, such as emergency alarms or security personnel.

- **Data-Driven Decision Making: Empowering Leaders with CAPS:** One of the most powerful features of the **Critical Aggression Prevention System (CAPS)** is its **data-driven approach** to decision-making. Through the **CAPS Dashboard**, organizations have access to real-time data and insights into the behavioral patterns of individuals across the organization. This enables leaders to make informed and strategic decisions regarding **safety protocols, staff training, and intervention strategies**.

   The **CAPS Dashboard** is fully forensic in nature, providing **longitudinal recordation** that tracks and monitors behaviors over time. This allows for continuous prevention efforts, as it can highlight trends and patterns that might otherwise go unnoticed. With this wealth of data, decision-makers can implement more effective safety measures and training initiatives, customized to the specific needs of their organization.

   An important tool within CAPS is the **Judicious Interview**, which helps to affirm whether a potential aggressor still harbors an intent to do harm. This interview process, informed by real-time data from the CAPS system, allows trained professionals to engage with individuals identified as potential risks and determine whether de-escalation has been successful. If the interview reveals that the individual no longer has an intent to cause harm, further interventions can be tailored accordingly, providing reassurance to the organization that the threat has been mitigated.

By leveraging the power of data, CAPS offers a level of **precision and reliability** that allows organizations to be proactive rather than reactive. The system ensures that every decision related to aggression management is based on **objective, real-time evidence**, allowing organizations to address potential threats before they escalate into incidents.

Certified Aggression Managers: Preventing Violence with Targeted Interventions

The role of **Certified Aggression Managers (CAMs)** is central to CAPS and its integration into organizational safety strategies. CAMs are trained not only to de-escalate potentially dangerous situations but also to **redirect aggression** in a way that benefits the aggressor and the organization. This advanced skill set plays a critical role in reducing conflict and maintaining a positive environment.

The Role of CAMs in Organizational Safety:

- **De-Escalation Skills**: CAMs are equipped with techniques for **de-escalating aggression** in real time, whether it's an emotional outburst from a student, a workplace argument between colleagues, or a patient's frustration in a healthcare setting. They understand how to **calm individuals down** and defuse situations before they become unmanageable.

- **Redirection of Aggression**: Beyond de-escalation, CAMs are trained to **redirect aggression**, helping aggressors see that their current behavior is not in their best interest and offering them a more constructive path. For instance, if an employee is engaged in **Cognitive Aggression**, such as manipulating colleagues or undermining authority, a CAM can step in to guide them toward more productive behaviors that achieve their goals without causing harm.

- **Proactive Environment Building**: CAMs are not only reactive—they are also proactive in identifying potential risks in an organization's culture and making recommendations to prevent aggression from taking root. This proactive approach helps organizations create a positive, collaborative environment that reduces the likelihood of conflict.

Building a Culture of Safety with CAPS

Organizations that successfully integrate CAPS into their broader safety strategies benefit from more than just reduced aggression—they also create a **culture of safety** that permeates every level of the organization. In this culture, aggression is identified early, addressed constructively, and prevented from escalating into serious conflicts.

This culture of safety does not just prevent violence—it also improves the organization's **team dynamics**, **employee satisfaction**, and overall **productivity**.

Steps to Building a Culture of Safety:

1. **Training and Empowerment**: Ensure that all personnel, from entry-level employees to senior leaders, are trained in CAPS principles. This includes recognizing early precursor-signs of aggression, understanding how to report behaviors, and knowing who to approach for intervention.

2. **Clear Reporting Channels**: Establish clear, confidential channels for reporting aggressive behavior. This can be done through the **CAPS Mobile App**, allowing staff to log behaviors discreetly and in real time. This encourages a culture of **openness and transparency**, where aggression is reported early.

3. **Regular Safety Audits**: Use the **CAPS Dashboard** to monitor patterns of behavior and conduct regular audits of the organization's safety measures. This data-driven approach helps identify potential risks before they escalate, ensuring that safety strategies are continuously updated.

4. **Leadership Buy-In**: Leadership commitment is crucial for creating a culture of safety. When leaders actively support CAPS and demonstrate that preventing aggression is a priority, it sends a message to the entire organization that safety and well-being are non-negotiable.

Certified Aggression Managers: Beyond Diffusion to Redirection

Let's revisit a critical concept from earlier: **Certified Aggression Managers** go beyond simply defusing aggressive situations. They have the advanced skill set necessary to **redirect an aggressor's behavior** in a way that not only de-escalates tension but also prevents future incidents.

When an aggressor is convinced that the path they are on will not serve their best interests, they are more likely to change their behavior. CAMs use **persuasion techniques**, offering alternative solutions that align with the aggressor's goals but steer them away from destructive actions.

This **redirection of aggression** is what makes CAPS truly unique. Rather than forcing an aggressor to back down, which can lead to resentment or future conflict, CAMs help aggressors find **self-motivated** reasons to change their behavior.

Compliance with Regulatory Requirements

One of the significant benefits of integrating CAPS into an organization's safety strategy is its **compliance** with key regulatory requirements. Whether it's **FERPA** in schools, **OSHA** in workplaces, or **HIPAA** in healthcare, CAPS operates within the boundaries of these regulations by focusing on **observable behaviors** and avoiding sensitive personal information.

For example, in a workplace setting, CAPS helps organizations comply with **OSHA regulations** on workplace violence prevention by providing a structured system for identifying and addressing early precursor-signs of aggression. In healthcare, CAPS ensures compliance with **HIPAA** by not requiring access to medical or psychological records, focusing instead on the observable actions of patients, staff, and visitors.

Conclusion: The Holistic Integration of CAPS into Organizational Safety

Integrating CAPS into an organization's broader safety strategy provides a **holistic approach** to aggression prevention. By focusing on early detection, data-driven insights, and real-time intervention, CAPS strengthens the organization's ability to prevent conflicts, improve

Chapter 12

communication, and create a positive environment where aggression is less likely to escalate.

The next chapter will focus on **case studies** from different sectors—education, healthcare, and corporate environments—that highlight how CAPS has been successfully integrated and the measurable impacts it has made in each setting.

Chapter 13

THE FUTURE OF CAPS: EVOLVING TO MEET NEW CHALLENGES

As organizations continue to face new and evolving challenges, the **Critical Aggression Prevention System (CAPS)** must also adapt to meet these demands. From the increasing use of **technology** in schools, workplaces, and healthcare to the growing complexity of social and behavioral issues, CAPS remains committed to staying at the forefront of aggression prevention. This chapter will explore how CAPS is evolving to tackle new threats, integrate with emerging technologies, and address the challenges of an ever-changing world.

Adapting to New Forms of Aggression: The Rise of Digital Harassment

One of the most significant changes in recent years has been the rise of **digital harassment** and **cyberbullying**. As more communication occurs online, both in schools and workplaces, aggressive behaviors are no longer limited to face-to-face interactions. Harassment, bullying, and discrimination are increasingly taking place over digital platforms such as social media, email, and instant messaging apps. This shift requires CAPS to adapt its methods to address these new forms of aggression.

The Problem:

Digital harassment can be difficult to detect because it often happens outside of traditional environments like classrooms or offices. Victims may be targeted after hours or on personal devices, making it challenging for schools and organizations to intervene. Furthermore, the anonymity and reach of the internet can amplify the harm caused by these behaviors, making them more difficult to control.

How CAPS is Evolving:

CAPS is expanding its focus to include **digital aggression** by training **Aggression First Observers (AFOs)** and **Certified Aggression Managers (CAMs)** to recognize signs of **online harassment** and **cyberbullying**. These signs might include changes in a student's or employee's behavior, such as social withdrawal, emotional distress, or reluctance to use digital devices.

In addition, CAPS is developing tools to integrate with **digital communication platforms**, allowing organizations to monitor behavior patterns across both in-person and online interactions. By adapting its methods to include online environments, CAPS can continue to provide early intervention and prevention in an increasingly digital world.

Example: At a high school in California, teachers began noticing a student, Maya, who was becoming withdrawn and anxious, avoiding her phone during class and lunch breaks. CAPS was already in place, and one of the teachers, trained as an AFO, logged Maya's behavior into the **CAPS Mobile App**. The **Certified Aggression Manager** then intervened and discovered that Maya was the target of cyberbullying, receiving hostile messages from classmates over social media. The CAM worked with the school to address the bullying both online and in person, preventing the situation from escalating.

Leveraging AI and Machine Learning for Predictive Aggression Prevention

As CAPS evolves, it is also integrating **artificial intelligence (AI)** and **machine learning** to improve its ability to **predict aggression** and intervene before it escalates. AI can analyze vast amounts of behavioral data, identify patterns, and make real-time predictions about potential aggression. This technology can help organizations take **preventive action** even earlier, offering a more sophisticated and proactive approach to aggression management.

The Problem:

Human observation alone can sometimes miss the early, subtle signs of aggression, especially in large organizations or schools with hundreds or thousands of individuals. AI and machine learning can augment the human element by analyzing data points that might otherwise be overlooked, improving the accuracy and speed of intervention.

How CAPS is Evolving:

CAPS is integrating AI tools to analyze behavioral patterns collected through the **CAPS Mobile App** and **CAPS Dashboard**. These AI algorithms will identify **early warning signs** of aggression based on previous cases and flag individuals who are at higher risk of escalating their behavior. By predicting aggression with greater accuracy, CAPS can help organizations intervene before behaviors become harmful.

Example: In a large corporate setting, an employee named Greg was showing early precursor-signs of **Cognitive Aggression**, such as subtle manipulation of colleagues and strategic undermining of a team leader. These behaviors were logged into CAPS, but without clear confrontation or overt aggression, the behaviors might have gone unnoticed. The AI algorithm, however, flagged the pattern based on previous data and alerted a **Certified Aggression Manager** to intervene. This early action prevented the situation from spiraling into a larger conflict that could have harmed team dynamics and productivity.

Addressing New Social and Cultural Challenges

As societies become more diverse, organizations are facing increased challenges around issues of **inclusion**, **equity**, and **diversity**. While diversity enriches environments, it can also lead to misunderstandings, microaggressions, and conflicts if not managed properly. CAPS must adapt to help organizations navigate these complex social dynamics, ensuring that aggression prevention efforts are inclusive and effective across different cultures and identities.

The Problem:

Microaggressions—subtle, often unintentional slights based on race, gender, or other identity factors—are becoming more recognized as harmful forms of aggression. These behaviors can be difficult to identify and address because they are often ingrained in social interactions or unconscious biases. However, left unchecked, they can escalate into more overt forms of aggression, harassment, or discrimination.

How CAPS is Evolving:

CAPS is expanding its training to include **cultural competency**, ensuring that **Aggression First Observers** and **Certified Aggression Managers** are able to recognize and address **microaggressions** and other culturally specific forms of aggression. This includes training on how to intervene in situations where aggression is driven by misunderstandings related to cultural differences, gender identities, or other factors.

CAPS is also developing specific modules for industries and sectors that face heightened challenges related to diversity and inclusion, such as healthcare, education, and large corporations with global teams.

Example: At a university in the Northeast, tensions had been rising between different cultural groups on campus. Subtle microaggressions—such as insensitive comments about language or assumptions based on ethnicity—were contributing to an environment of discomfort and alienation. CAPS was implemented, and **Certified Aggression Managers** worked with students and staff to address these microaggressions. Through education and early intervention, the university was able to improve the campus climate and prevent the tensions from escalating into larger conflicts.

Expanding CAPS into Global Applications

As organizations continue to expand globally, the need for aggression prevention systems that can operate across different cultures, languages, and regulatory environments becomes more pressing. CAPS is evolving to meet this demand by developing frameworks that can be **customized** for use in **international** contexts while still adhering to local regulations and cultural norms.

The Problem:

Aggression, harassment, and bullying manifest differently across cultures, and what may be considered an acceptable behavior in one country may be viewed as hostile in another. Additionally, global organizations must navigate differing laws and regulations regarding workplace safety, data privacy, and behavioral management.

How CAPS is Evolving:

CAPS is developing **customized frameworks** for international use, allowing organizations to adapt the system to their local environments while maintaining the core principles of early aggression detection and intervention. This includes ensuring that CAPS is compliant with **global data privacy laws**, such as **GDPR** in Europe, while still providing the behavioral insights needed for effective aggression management.

CAPS is also working to create **multilingual** training programs for AFOs and CAMs, ensuring that the system can be implemented in global teams where language barriers might otherwise hinder effective intervention.

Example: A multinational corporation with offices in the U.S., Europe, and Asia implemented CAPS to improve employee well-being and prevent workplace aggression. The company faced challenges in addressing cultural differences that sometimes led to misunderstandings and microaggressions between teams. CAPS was customized for each office's cultural and legal context, providing tailored training on how to recognize and respond to aggression in ways that were culturally appropriate. This helped reduce conflicts and fostered a more inclusive workplace culture across the organization.

The Future of CAPS: Looking Ahead

As CAPS continues to evolve, its focus on **early detection**, **technology integration**, and **cultural adaptability** will remain central to its mission. The system is designed to be flexible, scalable, and responsive to the ever-changing nature of aggression in modern environments. Whether in schools, workplaces, healthcare, or international organizations, CAPS is committed to preventing aggression and creating safer, more productive environments for all.

Looking Ahead, CAPS Will Focus On:

- **Enhanced AI and machine learning** for predictive aggression detection.
- **Increased integration with digital platforms** to monitor online aggression and cyberbullying.

- **Global scalability** with localized customization for international use.
- **Ongoing training updates** to address new forms of aggression and cultural challenges.
- **Collaboration with mental health professionals** to expand CAPS' scope in addressing mental health crises that may lead to aggressive behaviors.

Conclusion: CAPS as a Future-Ready Solution

CAPS is more than a system for managing current aggression—it is a forward-looking solution designed to meet the evolving needs of schools, workplaces, healthcare, and other organizations. As aggression becomes more complex and multifaceted, CAPS will continue to adapt, ensuring that it remains an effective tool for preventing harm and fostering safer, more inclusive environments.

In the next chapter, we'll delve into how CAPS can further collaborate with mental health professionals, ensuring a more holistic approach to aggression prevention and mental health support.

Chapter 14
COLLABORATING WITH MENTAL HEALTH PROFESSIONALS: A HOLISTIC APPROACH TO AGGRESSION PREVENTION

While the **Critical Aggression Prevention System (CAPS)** is a powerful tool for identifying and managing aggression, its full potential is realized when integrated with broader mental health support. **Mental health professionals** play a crucial role in understanding the underlying emotional and psychological factors that can drive aggression. By collaborating with these professionals, CAPS can provide a more **holistic approach** to preventing not only physical violence but also the emotional and psychological harm that often precedes it.

In this chapter, we explore how CAPS can work alongside mental health experts to address the root causes of aggression, ensure that those at risk receive the appropriate care, and create safer, healthier environments in schools, workplaces, and healthcare settings.

The Connection Between Mental Health and Aggression

Aggression is often the result of **unaddressed mental health issues**, such as anxiety, depression, trauma, or stress. In many cases, individuals who exhibit aggressive behavior are responding to underlying emotional distress that has gone unresolved. CAPS excels at identifying **early warning signs** of aggression, but mental health professionals can help address the **root causes** of these behaviors, providing the support and treatment necessary to prevent escalation.

The Problem:

Many schools and organizations face challenges in providing adequate mental health support. Mental health issues often go unrecognized or untreated, and those who exhibit aggressive behavior may not receive the help they need until it is too late. Without collaboration between CAPS and mental health professionals, the system may miss opportunities to address the **underlying emotional triggers** driving aggression.

How CAPS and Mental Health Professionals Work Together:

CAPS identifies the **pre-incident behavioral human-based precursor-signs of aggression**, such as irritability, withdrawal, or verbal outbursts, and logs these behaviors through the **CAPS Mobile App**. Once these behaviors are identified, CAPS trained mental health professionals—such as school counselors, psychologists, or social workers—can step in to assess whether the individual's aggression is linked to deeper emotional or psychological issues.

By collaborating with mental health professionals, **Certified Aggression Managers (CAMs)** can create a more comprehensive intervention plan that addresses both the **behavioral** and **emotional** aspects of aggression. This two-pronged approach ensures that individuals receive the support they need, reducing the likelihood of future incidents.

Example: At a middle school in Florida, a student named Jordan had been acting out in class, showing signs of Primal Aggression such as sudden outbursts and frequent conflicts with peers. A teacher, trained as an **Aggression First Observer (AFO)**, logged Jordan's behaviors into the CAPS system. The **Certified Aggression Manager** intervened and discovered that Jordan was struggling with anxiety and stress due to family issues at home. The CAM referred Jordan to the school counselor, who provided ongoing support and therapy. With this combined approach, Jordan's behavior improved significantly, and the school prevented a potential escalation into more serious aggression.

The Role of Mental Health Support in Schools

In schools, the importance of CAPS trained mental health support cannot be overstated. Students often face a variety of stressors, including academic pressure, social challenges, and personal trauma, which can manifest as aggressive behavior if left unaddressed. CAPS provides a framework for identifying students who are at risk, but mental health professionals are essential for providing the emotional support and counseling needed to help students cope with these challenges.

How CAPS Integrates with School Counseling:

- **Early Detection**: CAPS identifies early precursor-signs of emotional distress and aggression, such as changes in behavior or mood.

- **Collaboration with Counselors**: Once a student is flagged by CAPS, school counselors can assess the student's mental health needs, providing counseling or therapy as necessary.

- **Ongoing Support**: CAPS enables continuous monitoring of the student's behavior, allowing counselors to track progress and adjust support as needed.

By working together, CAPS and CAPS trained school counselors ensure that students are not only protected from the immediate risks of aggression but also receive long-term emotional support.

Supporting Employees' Mental Health in the Workplace

Workplace aggression is often linked to **workplace stress**, **burnout**, or **mental health issues** like anxiety or depression. In corporate settings, CAPS can play a crucial role in identifying employees who may be struggling with these issues before they escalate into conflict or aggression. By collaborating with **CAPS trained Employee Assistance Programs (EAPs)** and mental health professionals, CAPS can provide organizations with a comprehensive strategy for supporting employees' well-being and preventing aggression.

How CAPS and EAPs Work Together:

- **Identifying At-Risk Employees**: CAPS logs behavioral changes that may indicate stress, burnout, or emotional distress in employees. This information is shared with the company's EAP or HR team.

- **Referral to Mental Health Resources**: Employees who are identified as struggling with mental health issues can be referred to counseling, therapy, or stress management programs.

- **Creating a Supportive Workplace**: CAPS helps organizations foster a culture of well-being, where mental health is prioritized, and employees feel supported. This reduces the risk of aggression and improves overall productivity.

Example: In a large corporation, an employee named Lisa was showing signs of Cognitive Aggression, such as disengaging from team activities and displaying passive-aggressive behavior toward her colleagues. A colleague trained as an AFO logged these behaviors, and CAPS flagged Lisa for further assessment. The **Certified Aggression Manager** intervened and discovered that Lisa was experiencing severe burnout due to her workload. Lisa was referred to the company's CAPS trained EAP, where she received counseling and support for stress management. With the appropriate mental health support, Lisa's behavior improved, and the workplace conflict was resolved before it escalated.

Mental Health Support in Healthcare Settings

In healthcare environments, both **patients** and **staff** may experience aggression linked to emotional distress. Patients, particularly those in emergency or high-stress situations, may act out due to fear, frustration, or pain. Healthcare staff, in turn, may experience **burnout** or **compassion fatigue**, leading to workplace conflicts or emotional exhaustion. CAPS can help healthcare organizations identify these early precursor-signs of aggression and partner with mental health professionals to address the underlying causes.

How CAPS Works with Mental Health Teams in Healthcare:

- **Patient Behavior Monitoring**: CAPS tracks patient behaviors that indicate rising aggression, allowing healthcare professionals to intervene early and provide emotional support or psychiatric care.
- **Staff Support**: CAPS can also identify healthcare staff who are struggling with burnout or emotional distress, ensuring they receive the mental health care they need to prevent conflict or aggression in the workplace.

Example: In a hospital in New York, a nurse named Tom had been dealing with increasing emotional stress due to the demands of his job. Over time, Tom became short-tempered with colleagues and began showing signs of Primal Aggression, such as irritability and outbursts in high-stress situations. A fellow nurse, trained as an AFO, logged Tom's behavior into CAPS. The hospital's **Certified Aggression Manager** and HR team intervened, referring Tom to the hospital's mental health support services. With counseling and stress management support, Tom was able to regain emotional balance and improve his interactions with both colleagues and patients.

Creating a Holistic Approach to Aggression Prevention

By collaborating with mental health professionals, CAPS ensures that aggression prevention goes beyond simply managing behaviors—it addresses the **emotional and psychological needs** of individuals at risk. This holistic approach provides a more comprehensive solution to aggression, ensuring that students, employees, and patients receive the care they need to prevent further harm.

Key Benefits of Collaboration:

- **Early Intervention**: By identifying early precursor-signs of emotional distress, CAPS and mental health professionals can intervene before aggression escalates.

- **Long-Term Support**: Mental health professionals provide the counseling and therapy necessary to address the root causes of aggression, reducing the likelihood of future incidents.

- **Preventing Recurrence**: With ongoing support, individuals who have exhibited aggressive behavior are less likely to re-offend, creating safer environments in schools, workplaces, and healthcare facilities.

The Future of CAPS and Mental Health Collaboration

As CAPS continues to evolve, its collaboration with mental health professionals will become even more critical. By integrating **mental health assessments**, **stress management programs**, and **emotional support resources** alongside CAPS, organizations can create a **well-rounded**

safety strategy that addresses both the behavioral and emotional aspects of aggression.

In the future, CAPS can work more closely with mental health experts to develop new training programs that help Certified Aggression Managers recognize and address the mental health factors contributing to aggression. This will ensure that CAPS remains at the forefront of aggression prevention, providing comprehensive solutions for every environment.

Conclusion: A Holistic Solution for Aggression Prevention

CAPS' collaboration with mental health professionals allows for a more **holistic approach** to aggression prevention, one that addresses the emotional, psychological, and behavioral factors contributing to aggression. Whether in schools, workplaces, or healthcare facilities, this partnership ensures that individuals receive the support they need, creating safer, more supportive environments for everyone involved.

In the next chapter, we'll explore how CAPS can continue to innovate and adapt, focusing on the development of new tools, technologies, and approaches to further enhance its effectiveness in preventing aggression.

Chapter 15
CAPS INNOVATION: NEW TOOLS AND TECHNOLOGIES FOR THE FUTURE

The Future of CAPS: Innovation with Privacy at the Core

As the **Critical Aggression Prevention System (CAPS)** evolves, it continues to embrace **cutting-edge tools and technologies** that enhance its ability to detect, manage, and prevent aggression across a variety of environments—from schools and workplaces to healthcare facilities. The future of CAPS lies in its unwavering commitment to **innovation**, ensuring that the system remains **adaptable, effective, and scalable** to address emerging threats in a rapidly changing world.

However, a **foundational principle** of CAPS is that it **does not violate privacy regulations**. This commitment is central to the system's design and operation. **CAPS remains fully compliant with privacy laws** such as the **Health Insurance Portability and Accountability Act (HIPAA), Family Educational Rights and Privacy Act (FERPA)**, the **Civil Rights Act of 1964, and now California's Senate Bill 553 (Workplace Violence "Prevention" Program)**. CAPS focuses solely on **observable behaviors** in real-time interactions, without accessing personal medical or psychological records.

One of the most frequent questions I encounter is whether CAPS can be integrated with other platforms. While this might seem like a beneficial move, it's important to understand that doing so could potentially **compromise the integrity of CAPS data**. Integrating CAPS with other systems may inadvertently expose sensitive data, putting it at risk of violating HIPAA, FERPA, or the Civil Rights Act. Therefore, maintaining CAPS as a **standalone system** ensures that it continues to operate within its **proven, privacy-compliant framework**, offering maximum protection for both the individuals being monitored and the organization implementing the system.

By keeping CAPS independent, we preserve its **core strengths**: reliability, privacy, and precision in aggression management. As CAPS continues to evolve, its **commitment to innovation** will always be balanced by its **dedication to privacy** and legal compliance, making it the most effective and secure solution for aggression prevention.

This chapter explores the **new tools, technologies**, and **approaches** that CAPS is developing to ensure it stays ahead of the curve in **aggression prevention**. We will also revisit elements from the old Chapter 8 to highlight how CAPS will continue to leverage its core principles while embracing new innovations.

The Future of CAPS: Innovation Without Predictive Guarantees

One of the most significant advancements CAPS is focusing on is the use of **data analytics and machine learning** to predict and prevent aggressive behaviors. By analyzing large datasets and identifying patterns, CAPS can **anticipate when and where aggression is likely to occur**, allowing for **earlier intervention** and more effective prevention. However, it's important to clarify that CAPS is **not predictive in the sense of forecasting exact future behaviors**. For example, we do not claim that someone at Stage 4 will, in a week, progress to Stage 8 and commit violence.

That is **not what CAPS does**. Instead, CAPS identifies individuals at **Stage 4**, engages with them through proven techniques, and **redirects** them so that they never reach Stage 8. The focus is on **preventing escalation**, not predicting it. CAPS relies on identifying early precursor signs and using real-time data to prompt **immediate intervention**, ensuring the individual never gets to a critical point where violence is a likely outcome.

The Problem:

Aggression can be difficult to predict, as it manifests differently depending on the individual and environment. Without tools to recognize early signs, organizations may miss opportunities to intervene before situations escalate.

CAPS: Leveraging AI and Data Analytics for Enhanced Aggression Prevention:

As CAPS continues to evolve, one of the most exciting areas of development is to develop **enhanced data analytics tools**, which leverage behavioral data from the **CAPS Mobile App** and **Dashboard**. These tools can be designed to use **artificial intelligence (AI)** and **machine learning algorithms** to track behavior patterns and flag potential risks in real time.

For example, if a student, employee, or patient begins to show subtle changes in behavior—such as irritability, withdrawal, or increased anxiety—CAPS can immediately alert the appropriate personnel to intervene before the situation escalates. This system ensures that early signs of aggression are never overlooked, allowing for **proactive engagement** rather than reactive measures.

Beyond identifying individual behavior patterns, the enhanced tools in CAPS could potentially highlight broader **organizational trends**. For instance, if these behavioral changes are consistently observed within a particular department or group, it could prompt leadership to review **management practices** or other potential underlying issues that may be contributing to the increase in stress or aggression. By providing these **insights at both the individual and departmental level**, CAPS enables organizations to take a holistic approach to aggression management, addressing not only the behaviors themselves but also the possible systemic factors driving them.

This cutting-edge approach to behavior tracking and data analysis empowers organizations to remain **one step ahead** in preventing aggression, ensuring that interventions are timely and targeted.

This approach allows CAPS to go beyond merely reacting to aggression as it happens. By leveraging **real-time data**, CAPS enables proactive aggression prevention, providing the tools necessary to intervene early, and preventing the escalation of potentially harmful behaviors.

Example:
In a large high school, CAPS is implemented to track behavioral data

across the student population. Over time, the system identified that students facing academic pressure during final exams were more likely to exhibit aggressive behaviors. Armed with this data, the school can implement stress management workshops and mental health support during exam periods, reducing incidents of aggression by **30%**.

The CAPS Mobile App: Expanding Functionality

The **CAPS Mobile App** has been a critical tool for logging and tracking behaviors in real time, but its functionality is constantly being expanded to meet the needs of different environments. The future of the CAPS Mobile App will include new features designed to improve **user experience**, increase **data accuracy**, and integrate with other systems already in place within schools, workplaces, and healthcare facilities.

How CAPS is Innovating:

- **Advanced Reporting Features**: The CAPS Mobile App already has advanced reporting tools, allowing users to capture detailed behavioral data, including video, audio, and text-based notes. This ensures that observations are accurate and provide a fuller picture of the situation.

- **Geolocation Services**: The app will in the future include **geolocation services**, allowing organizations to track where incidents of aggression occur. This feature is especially useful in large environments such as schools or corporate campuses, where understanding the geography of aggressive incidents can help with planning and intervention.

CAPS Dashboard: A Central Hub for Behavioral Insights

The **CAPS Dashboard** is already a powerful tool for tracking, monitoring, and analyzing behaviors across an organization. As CAPS continues to innovate, the Dashboard will become even more essential as a **central hub** for **behavioral insights**, allowing users to visualize patterns and trends over time.

How CAPS is Innovating:

- **Customizable Data Views**: The CAPS Dashboard will allow users to customize their data views based on specific needs. Whether tracking individual behaviors, team dynamics, or organizational trends, the Dashboard will provide a **tailored experience** that delivers the most relevant insights.

- **Real-Time Alerts**: CAPS Dashboard already include **real-time alerts** that notify CAPS trained administrators, Certified Aggression Managers (CAMs), and CAPS trained mental health professionals of any significant changes in behavior patterns. These alerts ensure that interventions can happen immediately, preventing aggression from escalating.

- **Advanced Analytics and AI Integration**: By integrating **AI-powered analytics**, the Dashboard will in the future be able to highlight emerging trends and provide actionable recommendations for addressing aggression. For example, the system might suggest specific interventions or training programs based on patterns identified across the organization.

Example: In a large corporation, the CAPS Dashboard can be used to track employee behaviors across multiple departments. Over time, the system identified that a particular team was experiencing higher levels of interpersonal conflict. Based on this data, the **Certified Aggression Manager** implemented a series of team-building exercises and communication workshops, which significantly reduced aggression and improved team morale.

Virtual Reality (VR) Training for Certified Aggression Managers

As CAPS continues to push the boundaries of aggression prevention, it is exploring the use of **virtual reality (VR)** to enhance training for **Certified Aggression Managers**. VR allows for immersive training experiences that replicate real-world scenarios, providing CAMs with the opportunity to practice their skills in a safe and controlled environment.

How CAPS is Innovating:

- **Immersive De-Escalation Scenarios**: CAMs will be able to participate in immersive de-escalation training, where they practice handling aggressive individuals in virtual environments that mimic real-world situations, such as classrooms, offices, or healthcare settings.

- **Interactive Role-Playing**: Interactive Role-Playing and Global Application of CAPS VR As part of its ongoing innovation, CAPS is developing a **Virtual Reality (VR) system** that will include **interactive role-playing features**. This technology allows **Certified Aggression Managers (CAMs)** to engage in simulated conversations with aggressors, providing a safe environment to practice techniques for **calming individuals** and **redirecting aggressive behavior**.

    Through this immersive experience, CAMs will be able to refine their skills in real-world scenarios without the immediate pressures of a live situation. The system simulates a variety of situations and personalities, offering CAMs valuable experience in **handling high-stress interactions** with precision and confidence.

    Looking ahead, the VR system will eventually have the capability to work **across international boundaries**, enabling global employers to adopt CAPS as a **universal approach** to workplace safety. By using a common platform for training, organizations around the world will be able to **standardize their aggression management practices**, creating safer environments regardless of cultural or geographic differences. This technology will help bridge the gap between countries and industries, allowing for a **cohesive, global solution** to aggression prevention.

- **Feedback and Evaluation**: The VR training system will provide real-time feedback and evaluation, allowing CAMs to assess their performance and improve their de-escalation techniques.

Example: At a university, new **Certified Aggression Managers** can undergo VR training before taking on their roles. They participated in simulations of aggressive student behaviors, such as verbal altercations during classroom discussions or disputes in residence halls. The immersive training helped them practice their intervention skills and receive real-time feedback, significantly improving their confidence and effectiveness when managing real-world incidents.

Expanding CAPS to Digital and Remote Environments

As remote work and digital communication become more prevalent, aggression is increasingly taking place online. CAPS is expanding its focus to include **digital environments**, ensuring that aggressive behaviors in remote or virtual settings are just as effectively identified and managed as those in physical spaces.

The Problem:

With the rise of remote work and digital communication platforms, aggression now manifests in **virtual meetings**, **emails**, and **chat systems**. These environments can make it harder to identify and intervene in cases of aggression, especially when behaviors are subtle or spread out across time zones and locations.

How CAPS is Innovating:

CAPS is considering tools to track and manage aggression in **digital communication platforms**, such as remote collaboration tools, email systems, and chat platforms. These tools will allow organizations to monitor behavior in virtual spaces and intervene when signs of aggression are detected.

- **Digital Aggression Detection**: CAPS will be able to analyze communication patterns, identifying aggressive language, passive-aggressive behaviors, or exclusionary tactics in remote work environments.

- **Remote Interventions**: Certified Aggression Managers will be equipped with tools to intervene in digital settings, such as conducting virtual mediation sessions or offering conflict resolution resources for remote teams.

Example: In a global corporation, remote teams experienced increasing conflicts during virtual meetings and project collaborations. CAPS will be able to be implemented to monitor communication patterns across the organization's digital platforms. The system flagged several instances of passive-aggressive behavior during team meetings, and a **Certified Aggression Manager** conducted a virtual intervention to resolve the conflict. This remote intervention prevented the conflict from escalating and improved team collaboration.

Conclusion: Innovating for a Safer Future

The future of CAPS is defined by **innovation**—from leveraging predictive analytics and AI to expanding functionality in digital environments and using VR to enhance training, CAPS remains at the forefront of aggression prevention. By continuing to embrace new technologies and tools, CAPS ensures that it can address the ever-evolving nature of aggression, creating safer, more productive environments across schools, workplaces, healthcare facilities, and beyond.

In the next chapter, we'll explore the broader **impact of CAPS** on organizational culture and how this system can foster **long-term behavioral change**, improving not only safety but also the overall well-being of individuals in every environment.

Chapter 16

FOSTERING LONG-TERM BEHAVIORAL CHANGE AND ORGANIZATIONAL CULTURE WITH CAPS

The **Critical Aggression Prevention System (CAPS)** does more than just prevent isolated incidents of aggression—it has the power to create lasting **behavioral change** and transform the **culture** of entire organizations. By focusing on **early intervention, collaborative training**, and **ongoing support**, CAPS helps individuals and organizations not only address immediate concerns but also foster a culture of respect, safety, and productivity.

This chapter explores how CAPS promotes **long-term behavioral change**, helps organizations create a culture that prioritizes safety and well-being, and reinforces positive behaviors over time. We'll also revisit ideas from the old Chapter 9 to highlight how CAPS drives both individual and systemic change.

CAPS as a Driver of Behavioral Change

At its core, CAPS is built on the premise that **early intervention** and **consistent reinforcement** of positive behaviors can prevent aggression from escalating into more serious conflicts. By identifying early precursor-signs of both **Primal** and **Cognitive Aggression**, CAPS provides organizations with the tools they need to address these behaviors at their roots, fostering positive change over the long term.

The Problem:

Many traditional approaches to managing aggression focus on **reacting** to incidents after they occur, which often leads to temporary solutions without addressing the underlying causes. Without a proactive system like CAPS, organizations may struggle to create lasting change, leaving them vulnerable to recurring incidents of aggression, bullying, harassment, or discrimination.

Chapter 16

How CAPS Drives Behavioral Change:

CAPS uses **data-driven insights** and **real-time interventions** to influence behavior at every level of an organization. By teaching individuals to recognize and modify their own behaviors early on, CAPS encourages them to adopt more constructive ways of managing conflict. Certified Aggression Managers (CAMs) are equipped with the skills to not only de-escalate situations but also to **redirect** aggression in ways that benefit the individual and the organization.

Through a combination of ongoing monitoring, coaching, and support, CAPS fosters an environment where individuals learn to identify and address their own aggressive tendencies, promoting self-awareness and long-term behavioral change.

Example: In a large corporate setting, several employees in a high-pressure sales department were prone to aggressive behaviors during quarterly reviews, such as publicly criticizing colleagues or undermining others' work. After implementing CAPS, Certified Aggression Managers held regular **coaching sessions** with team leaders to help them recognize these behaviors early. Over time, employees learned to provide constructive feedback rather than resorting to aggressive tactics, leading to a more positive and productive team dynamic.

Creating a Culture of Prevention and Respect

One of the most powerful impacts of CAPS is its ability to shift an organization's culture toward **prevention** rather than **reaction**. By embedding CAPS into the fabric of an organization, leadership can promote a culture that values **trust, respect, collaboration**, and **empathy**. This cultural shift not only prevents aggression but also improves overall morale, trust, and engagement.

How CAPS Promotes Cultural Change:

- **Training and Awareness**: CAPS provides **training programs** that educate all members of an organization on how to identify, prevent, and address aggression. This training fosters a shared understanding of behavioral expectations and creates a sense of collective responsibility for maintaining a safe and supportive environment.

- **Reinforcing Positive Behavior**: CAPS reinforces positive behaviors by recognizing and rewarding constructive actions, such as effective communication, conflict resolution, and collaboration. This helps to shift the focus from punitive measures to **positive reinforcement**, encouraging individuals to model respectful behavior.

- **Leadership Commitment**: When leaders actively support CAPS and demonstrate their commitment to preventing aggression, it sets a powerful example for the rest of the organization. Leaders play a crucial role in shaping the culture, and their engagement with CAPS helps to normalize early intervention and open communication.

Sustaining Behavioral Change with Ongoing Support

For behavioral change to be sustained over time, organizations must provide **ongoing support** and ensure that CAPS remains integrated into their daily operations. This involves regular **retraining**, **evaluation**, and **adjustment** of CAPS strategies to reflect the evolving needs of the organization.

Ongoing Support Strategies:

- **Continuous Training and Development**: CAPS provides regular opportunities for staff to refresh their skills and deepen their understanding of aggression prevention. Whether through **online courses**, **workshops**, or **virtual reality training**, ongoing development ensures that individuals stay equipped to handle new challenges.

- **Monitoring and Feedback**: The **CAPS Mobile App** and **Dashboard** offer continuous monitoring of behaviors, allowing organizations to identify emerging trends and address them before they escalate. Regular feedback sessions between CAMs, AFOs, and leadership help to fine-tune interventions and maintain a focus on long-term change.

- **Recognition of Progress**: CAPS encourages organizations to celebrate positive behavioral changes by recognizing individuals and teams that exemplify trust, respect, collaboration, and effective aggression management. This recognition helps reinforce the cultural shift toward positive behaviors.

Impact on Individual and Team Performance

By fostering a culture of prevention, trust, and respect, CAPS not only reduces aggression but also has a positive impact on individual and team performance. When aggression is effectively managed, individuals feel safer, more supported, and more engaged in their work, which leads to higher **teamwork, leadership, loyalty, productivity**, **profitability**, and **morale**.

How CAPS Improves Performance:

- **Reduced Aggression and thus Conflict**: When individuals are trained to recognize and manage aggression early, issues are resolved before they become conflict, leading to a more harmonious and productive work or learning environment.

- **Enhanced Communication**: CAPS promotes **open communication**, which helps teams collaborate more effectively and resolve misunderstandings before they become sources of tension.

- **Increased Engagement**: When individuals feel that their safety and well-being are prioritized, they are more likely to be engaged and invested in their work. This leads to improved job satisfaction and overall performance.

The Role of Leadership in Sustaining Change

Leadership is essential for sustaining the long-term benefits of CAPS. When leaders actively participate in CAPS training, model respectful behavior, and prioritize aggression prevention, they set the tone for the entire organization. Their commitment ensures that CAPS is not seen as a temporary initiative but as a permanent part of the organization's culture.

Leadership's Role in CAPS:

- **Championing CAPS**: Leaders who champion CAPS and regularly communicate its importance help build buy-in from all members of the organization. This includes hosting training sessions, using the **CAPS Dashboard** to track progress, and celebrating success stories.

- **Allocating Resources**: Effective implementation of CAPS requires resources, including time for training, investment in technology, and support for Certified Aggression Managers. Leaders must ensure that CAPS is adequately supported so that it can continue to drive long-term change.

- **Leading by Example**: Leaders must model the behaviors they want to see in their teams. By consistently demonstrating respectful communication, preventing conflict, and early intervention, leaders reinforce the values that CAPS promotes.

Conclusion: CAPS as a Long-Term Solution for Behavioral Change

CAPS is not just a reactive system for managing immediate conflicts—it is a long-term solution for fostering **positive behavioral change** and creating a culture of respect and safety. By embedding CAPS into an organization's daily operations, providing ongoing support, and ensuring leadership engagement, organizations can build environments where aggression is prevented before it starts, and positive behaviors are reinforced over time.

In the next chapter, we will look at the measurable outcomes that organizations have achieved through CAPS and how these results demonstrate the system's effectiveness in preventing aggression, improving safety, and promoting well-being.

This page intentionally left blank

Chapter 17

MEASURABLE OUTCOMES: THE IMPACT OF CAPS ON SAFETY, WELL-BEING, AND PRODUCTIVITY

The **Critical Aggression Prevention System (CAPS)** has proven to be a transformative tool for preventing aggression, fostering long-term behavioral change, and enhancing organizational culture. In this chapter, we will focus on the **measurable outcomes** that CAPS has achieved across various environments—schools, workplaces, and healthcare settings. These results demonstrate how CAPS not only prevents aggression but also significantly improves **safety**, **well-being**, and **productivity** for individuals and organizations alike.

We'll also revisit elements from the old Chapter 9 to highlight how CAPS can quantify success, providing organizations with clear data that showcases the system's effectiveness in preventing violence and creating positive environments.

The Importance of Measuring Success with CAPS

One of the key benefits of CAPS is its ability to track, monitor, and evaluate the effectiveness of its interventions. By using the **CAPS Dashboard**, organizations can access real-time data on behaviors, incidents, and interventions, which allows for a more **data-driven** approach to aggression prevention. This data can be used to measure success, adjust strategies, and demonstrate the impact CAPS is having on an organization's culture and performance.

How CAPS Measures Success:

- **Reduction in Aggressive Incidents**: CAPS tracks the number of reported incidents of aggression, conflict, sexual harassment, bullying, and other negative behaviors. By comparing data over time, organizations can see clear reductions in these incidents as CAPS interventions take effect.

- **Improvement in Team Dynamics**: CAPS monitors improvements in communication, collaboration, and conflict resolution within teams, which are key indicators of a healthier organizational culture.

- **Employee and Student Well-Being**: CAPS data can be correlated with other metrics, such as employee or student surveys, to track improvements in **well-being** and **engagement**. As aggression decreases, individuals feel safer and more supported in their environments.

Reduction in Workplace Violence and Aggression

CAPS has proven to be highly effective in reducing incidents of **workplace violence** and **aggression**, particularly in industries that are prone to high levels of stress, such as healthcare, manufacturing, and corporate environments. By identifying early precursor-signs of aggression and providing tools for de-escalation, CAPS has helped organizations protect their employees and create safer work environments.

Measurable Impact of CAPS in Workplaces:

- **Decrease in Workplace Violence**: Organizations that implement CAPS typically see a significant reduction in workplace violence and harassment incidents. This is achieved through early intervention and better management of stress, conflict, and emotional triggers.

- **Improved Employee Morale and Retention**: As workplace aggression decreases, employee morale and job satisfaction increase. Employees are more likely to stay in an organization that prioritizes their safety and well-being, leading to higher retention rates.

- **Cost Savings**: Reducing incidents of aggression and violence also leads to cost savings. CAPS helps organizations avoid the costs associated with workplace violence, such as legal fees, workers' compensation claims, and lost productivity.

Increased Student and Staff Safety in Schools

One of CAPS' most significant areas of impact has been in **educational settings**, where the system has been used to reduce **bullying**, **harassment**, and **school violence**. By creating safer learning environments, CAPS not only prevents aggression but also improves academic outcomes, emotional well-being, and staff-student relationships.

Measurable Impact of CAPS in Schools:

- **Reduction in Bullying and Harassment**: Schools using CAPS have consistently reported fewer incidents of bullying and harassment. This is due to early detection of the subtle signs of aggression, which allows for timely intervention.

- **Improved Academic Performance**: When students feel safe and supported, their academic performance improves. CAPS data shows that schools with reduced aggression see better attendance rates, higher grades, and improved overall student achievement.

- **Positive School Climate**: CAPS fosters a culture of respect, collaboration, and open communication. Surveys of students and staff in schools with CAPS consistently show higher levels of satisfaction with the school environment.

Impact on Healthcare Environments: Reducing Patient and Staff Aggression

Healthcare facilities are often high-stress environments where both patients and staff can experience aggression. CAPS has been particularly effective in healthcare settings, where it helps reduce the **non-fatal assaults** and **verbal abuse** that healthcare workers frequently encounter. By identifying and addressing these behaviors early, CAPS helps create safer healthcare environments.

Measurable Impact of CAPS in Healthcare:

- **Reduction in Patient Aggression**: Healthcare facilities using CAPS report fewer incidents of patient aggression toward staff, particularly in emergency rooms and high-stress departments. Early intervention and de-escalation help prevent these incidents from escalating into physical violence.

- **Improved Staff Retention**: Reducing aggression and workplace violence improves staff morale and retention in healthcare facilities. Healthcare workers are more likely to stay in environments where they feel safe and supported.

- **Improved Patient Care**: When aggression is effectively managed, healthcare staff are better able to focus on providing high-quality patient care. This leads to improved patient satisfaction and outcomes.

Improved Organizational Performance

By fostering a culture of **prevention**, **early intervention**, and **respect**, CAPS has a measurable impact on organizational performance across all sectors. Whether in schools, workplaces, or healthcare settings, CAPS helps organizations improve **communication**, **team dynamics**, and **overall productivity**.

Measurable Organizational Benefits of CAPS:

- **Enhanced Productivity**: When individuals feel safe and supported, they are more engaged and productive. CAPS has been shown to increase productivity by reducing workplace conflicts and improving team collaboration.

- **Stronger Team Dynamics**: CAPS encourages open communication and proactive conflict resolution, which leads to stronger team dynamics and more effective collaboration.

- **Positive Organizational Culture**: CAPS helps organizations create a culture that prioritizes safety, respect, and well-being. This culture shift leads to higher employee or student satisfaction, better performance, and a more positive overall environment.

Long-Term Results: CAPS as a Permanent Solution

One of the most important outcomes of CAPS is its ability to produce **long-term results**. By embedding CAPS into the fabric of an organization's culture, leadership ensures that the system continues to prevent aggression, improve safety, and foster positive behavioral change over time. The results of CAPS are not temporary—they are **sustained** through ongoing training, monitoring, and adaptation to new challenges.

Key Long-Term Outcomes of CAPS:

- **Sustained Reductions in Aggression**: Over time, CAPS leads to lasting reductions in incidents of aggression, bullying, harassment, and workplace violence.

- **Cultural Transformation**: Organizations that consistently use CAPS experience a **cultural shift** toward prevention, early intervention, and mutual respect.

- **Continued Improvement**: As CAPS evolves with new tools and technologies, organizations can continue to improve their safety and well-being efforts, ensuring that they remain proactive in addressing emerging challenges.

Conclusion: The Proven Impact of CAPS

The measurable outcomes of CAPS demonstrate its effectiveness as a **proactive solution** for preventing aggression and improving safety, well-being, and productivity. Across schools, workplaces, and healthcare settings, CAPS delivers long-term results that go beyond simply reducing conflict—it transforms cultures, enhances performance, and creates environments where individuals can thrive.

In the next chapter, we'll explore the future of CAPS, including how it can continue to adapt and evolve to meet the needs of a rapidly changing world.

This page intentionally left blank

Chapter 18
THE FUTURE OF CAPS: ADAPTING TO A RAPIDLY CHANGING WORLD

As the **Critical Aggression Prevention System (CAPS)** continues to evolve, its mission to prevent aggression and violence remains as crucial as ever. However, the world is changing rapidly, and CAPS must adapt to address new challenges, technologies, and social dynamics. In this chapter, we will explore the future of CAPS—how it will continue to innovate, expand its capabilities, and meet the demands of an increasingly complex and interconnected world.

Drawing on ideas throughout this book, we'll look at the **global expansion** of CAPS, its role in addressing new forms of aggression, and the ways in which it can further contribute to building safer, more inclusive environments.

Global Expansion: CAPS Beyond Borders

In an increasingly interconnected world, aggression is not limited by geographical boundaries. As organizations become more global and culturally diverse, the need for a system like CAPS that can adapt to different cultural contexts and legal frameworks is paramount. The future of CAPS includes **global expansion**, where the system can be tailored to address aggression in **multinational corporations**, **schools**, and **healthcare systems** around the world.

Challenges of Global Implementation:

- **Adapting CAPS to Diverse Environments**: Different cultures have different norms around communication, conflict, and aggression. CAPS must be adaptable to the cultural nuances of each region while maintaining its core principles of early detection and prevention. Remembering the CAPS is built on a human-based platform, it can apply anywhere where there are humans, regardless of their culture.

- **Compliance with Local Regulations**: As **CAPS** continues to expand its global reach, it must navigate the **legal frameworks** of various countries, particularly regarding **privacy, workplace safety, and data protection**. Each nation has its own set of regulations, such as **GDPR** (General Data Protection Regulation) in Europe, that must be followed to ensure the system remains compliant while delivering the insights necessary for effective aggression prevention.

  One of the key advantages of CAPS is that it does not rely on sensitive personal attributes such as **culture, gender, education, age, sexual orientation, religion**, or **mental health assessments** to function. Instead, CAPS tracks **observable behaviors** that are universally applicable, without infringing on privacy or protected categories. This design helps ensure that CAPS remains compliant with stringent regulations like GDPR, while also avoiding potential legal challenges in other regions.

  By maintaining a focus on behavior-based data and avoiding the collection of personal identifiers that could conflict with local laws, CAPS ensures that its approach to aggression prevention remains **both effective and legally sound**. This flexibility not only allows for smooth implementation across different countries and industries but also **guarantees compliance** with a wide array of privacy and data protection laws around the world.

- **Language and Accessibility**: CAPS will expand its **multilingual capabilities**, ensuring that the system can be used in different languages and is accessible to individuals from diverse backgrounds.

How CAPS is Preparing for Global Expansion:

CAPS is developing **customizable frameworks** for different cultural and legal environments. By working with local experts and organizations, CAPS will ensure that its tools and strategies can be effectively integrated into **international contexts** without losing their core effectiveness.

Addressing Emerging Forms of Aggression

As technology advances and society changes, new forms of aggression are emerging. **Cyberbullying**, **digital harassment**, and **remote work conflicts** are becoming more prevalent, requiring CAPS to evolve to address these issues. The future of CAPS includes expanding its capabilities to track and manage aggression in both **physical** and **digital** spaces.

Challenges of Digital Aggression:

- **Anonymity and Scale**: Digital platforms allow individuals to engage in aggressive behaviors anonymously and on a larger scale, making it more difficult to track and intervene.

- **Blurring of Boundaries**: In remote work environments, the lines between professional and personal interactions can become blurred, leading to new types of conflicts that may be harder to detect.

How CAPS is Evolving to Address Digital Aggression:

CAPS is considering expanding its focus to include tools that monitor and track aggression in **digital environments**. This includes the ability to analyze communication patterns in virtual meetings, email systems, and social media, as well as providing **Certified Aggression Managers (CAMs)** with the tools they need to manage conflicts that arise in these spaces.

Integration of Advanced Technologies: AI, Machine Learning, and VR

The future of CAPS will see greater integration of **artificial intelligence (AI)**, **machine learning**, and **virtual reality (VR)** technologies to enhance its ability to prevent aggression. These technologies will enable CAPS to become even more proactive and effective in identifying early precursor-signs of aggression and providing real-time interventions.

CAPS in New Sectors: Expanding Beyond Traditional Environments

As CAPS continues to evolve, it has the potential to expand beyond traditional environments such as schools, workplaces, and healthcare facilities. CAPS can be adapted for use in **public spaces, government institutions, transportation systems,** and other areas where aggression and conflict may occur.

How CAPS Can Be Adapted to New Sectors:

- **Public Spaces**: CAPS can be used in **public transportation** systems, **shopping malls**, and other communal areas to prevent conflicts between individuals in these high-traffic environments.

- **Government Institutions**: CAPS can be integrated into **government offices** and **public service environments** to manage aggression toward public servants and officials, ensuring their safety and well-being.

- **Law Enforcement**: CAPS has the potential to be adapted for use in **law enforcement** settings, helping officers identify and manage aggressive behavior before it escalates into violence.

Example: In a large urban transportation system, CAPS can be implemented to monitor aggression in subway stations and buses. By training station managers and security personnel as **Aggression First Observers** and **Certified Aggression Managers**, the system was able to reduce incidents of conflict between passengers and staff. CAPS provided real-time data on where and when incidents were most likely to occur, allowing the transportation authority to allocate resources more effectively and prevent escalation.

CAPS as a Tool for Promoting Equity and Inclusion

As CAPS continues to evolve, it will also play an increasingly important role in promoting **equity** and **inclusion** in schools, workplaces, and other environments. Aggression, harassment, and discrimination are often rooted in systemic issues related to race, gender, and other identity factors. CAPS can help organizations address these issues by providing tools for recognizing and preventing **microaggressions** and creating more inclusive environments.

How CAPS Promotes Equity and Inclusion:

- **Identifying Microaggressions**: CAPS can be used to track subtle forms of aggression, such as microaggressions based on race, gender, or other identity factors. Early detection allows organizations to address these issues before they escalate.

- **Supporting Inclusive Environments**: CAPS helps organizations create cultures of respect and inclusion by promoting open communication and proactive conflict resolution. This leads to more inclusive environments where all individuals feel safe and valued.

CAPS as a Global Leader in Aggression Prevention

As CAPS continues to innovate and expand, it has the potential to become a global leader in **aggression prevention**. By integrating advanced technologies, adapting to new forms of aggression, and expanding into diverse sectors, CAPS will remain at the forefront of creating safer, more inclusive environments across the world.

Future Vision for CAPS:

- **Global Reach**: CAPS will continue to expand into international markets, providing organizations around the world with the tools they need to prevent aggression and promote well-being.

- **Cutting-Edge Technology**: CAPS will leverage AI, machine learning, and VR to provide even more advanced solutions for identifying and managing aggression.

Conclusion: The Future of CAPS is Bright

The future of CAPS is one of continued **innovation, global expansion,** and **adaptation** to new challenges. As technology advances and society changes, CAPS will remain a critical tool for preventing aggression, promoting safety, and fostering inclusive environments. By staying ahead of emerging trends and integrating new technologies, CAPS will continue to provide organizations with the solutions they need to create safer, more productive, and more inclusive environments for everyone.

In the final chapter, we will explore how organizations can implement CAPS effectively and ensure its long-term success in preventing aggression and creating positive cultural change.

Chapter 19

Implementing CAPS for Long-Term Success: A Guide for Organizations & Institutions

Successfully implementing the **Critical Aggression Prevention System (CAPS)** requires a strategic approach that ensures the system is integrated into an organization's culture, operations, and long-term goals. In this chapter, we'll provide a comprehensive guide for organizations looking to adopt CAPS, covering the key steps for successful implementation, long-term maintenance, and maximizing the system's impact.

Drawing from the ideas of the old Chapter 12, we will discuss the importance of leadership commitment, employee engagement, ongoing training, and data-driven decision-making in ensuring CAPS is not just a short-term solution but a **sustained strategy** for preventing aggression and fostering positive environments.

Step 1: Leadership Commitment and Strategic Alignment

The first and most critical step in implementing CAPS is securing **leadership commitment**. Leadership plays a pivotal role in setting the tone for the organization's and institution's culture, and their active support of CAPS is essential for its success. Leaders must not only endorse CAPS but also demonstrate their commitment to creating an environment where aggression is prevented, and safety is prioritized.

How to Secure Leadership Commitment:

- **Align with Organizational & Institutional Goals**: Show how CAPS aligns with the organization's & Institutional broader goals, such as improving safety, reducing workplace conflicts, enhancing team dynamics, or promoting equity and inclusion.

- **Highlight the Benefits**: Emphasize the measurable outcomes of CAPS, such as reduced incidents of aggression, improved employee or student well-being, and cost savings from avoiding workplace violence and turnover.

- **Involve Leadership in Training**: Ensure that leaders undergo CAPS training themselves. This allows them to understand the system's value firsthand and model positive behaviors for the rest of the organization or institution.

Example: In a large healthcare organization, leadership committed to CAPS after seeing the system's ability to reduce workplace violence. The CEO and senior leaders participated in **Certified Aggression Manager (CAM)** training, which not only helped them understand how CAPS worked but also sent a strong message to employees that aggression prevention was a top priority for the organization.

Step 2: Building a CAPS Implementation Team

For a successful rollout, organizations or institutions should establish a dedicated **CAPS Implementation Team** responsible for overseeing the system's integration into daily operations. This team should include representatives from different areas of the organization, such as HR, security, leadership, and mental health support, to ensure a holistic approach.

Key Roles in the CAPS Implementation Team:

- **Certified Aggression Managers (CAMs)**: Trained to de-escalate aggression and manage conflicts, CAMs are central to the system's success. They will be the primary responders when aggression is identified.

- **Aggression First Observers (AFOs)**: These individuals, trained to identify early precursor-signs of aggression, will act as the eyes and ears on the ground, logging incidents through the **CAPS Mobile App** and alerting CAMs when necessary.

- **IT and Data Experts**: To ensure CAPS is seamlessly integrated with existing technology platforms (e.g., HR systems, security software), the IT team must be involved in the technical setup and ongoing data management.

Example: A university in New York assembled a cross-functional **CAPS Implementation Team** that included representatives from student affairs, campus security, IT, and faculty members. This team collaborated to implement CAPS across different departments, ensuring that both staff and students were trained in aggression prevention and the system was integrated with existing campus safety initiatives.

Step 3: Comprehensive CAPS Training

Training is essential to the successful implementation of CAPS. Organizations & Institutions must provide comprehensive training to all personnel, ensuring that everyone understands how to recognize, report, and manage aggression using the system's tools.

Key Components of CAPS Training:

- **Aggression Continuum**: Train staff to understand the stages of aggression, from early triggers to escalation, and how to intervene before situations become dangerous.

- **Using the CAPS Mobile App**: Provide hands-on training in using the app to log and report behaviors in real time. Ensure that staff feel comfortable with the technology and understand how to use it effectively.

- **De-escalation and Conflict Resolution**: Equip staff, especially CAMs, with practical de-escalation techniques and strategies for managing both **Primal** and **Cognitive Aggression**.

Example: At a corporate office in California, CAPS training was provided to all employees in the form of workshops, online courses, and hands-on practice with the **CAPS Mobile App**. Employees learned how to recognize subtle signs of aggression, log incidents, and escalate reports to Certified Aggression Managers. Regular follow-up training sessions ensured that staff stayed updated on best practices for aggression management.

Step 4: Integration with Existing Systems and Processes

To ensure that CAPS is effective, it must be fully integrated into the organization's existing systems and processes. This includes connecting

CAPS to security platforms, HR systems, and any other tools already in use for managing employee or student behavior, safety, and performance.

How to Integrate CAPS into Daily Operations:

- **Security and HR Collaboration**: CAPS should be connected to existing security systems to allow for seamless monitoring of incidents. HR should also be involved in managing reports and coordinating responses to behavioral concerns.

- **Data Integration**: CAPS' data should be integrated into the organization's broader data systems. This allows leadership to track trends, make informed decisions, and measure the impact of CAPS on organizational safety and well-being.

Example: At a large financial services company, CAPS was integrated with the organization's **HR performance management system**, allowing HR to track behavioral reports alongside other performance metrics. This data integration provided a more comprehensive view of employee well-being and helped HR proactively address issues before they escalated.

Step 5: Ongoing Monitoring, Feedback, and Improvement

To sustain the success of CAPS, organizations must establish processes for **ongoing monitoring** and **feedback**. This ensures that the system remains effective over time and continues to adapt to the organization's evolving needs.

Monitoring and Feedback Strategies:

- **Regular Data Reviews**: Use the **CAPS Dashboard** to monitor behavior patterns and trends. Regularly review data on incidents, interventions, and outcomes to identify areas for improvement.

- **Feedback Loops**: Establish channels for staff and students to provide feedback on their experience with CAPS. This feedback can be used to refine training, improve response times, and address any gaps in the system.

- **Continuous Training**: Offer refresher courses and advanced training opportunities to keep staff engaged and ensure that their skills remain sharp.

Example: A hospital in Florida conducted quarterly reviews of its **CAPS data** to track patient-related aggression and staff interventions. Based on the data, the hospital adjusted its training programs and added more resources to high-risk areas, such as the emergency department, resulting in a sustained reduction in aggressive incidents.

Step 6: Measuring and Reporting Success

The long-term success of CAPS can be measured through key performance indicators (KPIs) that demonstrate its impact on organizational safety, culture, and well-being. Leadership should regularly review these metrics and share success stories to maintain momentum and support for the system.

Key Metrics for Measuring CAPS Success:

- **Reduction in Aggression**: Track the number of aggressive incidents over time to demonstrate how CAPS is reducing violence, bullying, harassment, and workplace conflict.

- **Employee or Student Well-Being**: Use surveys and feedback tools to measure improvements in employee or student satisfaction, safety perceptions, and overall well-being.

- **Cost Savings**: Calculate the cost savings associated with reducing workplace violence, such as lower turnover rates, reduced legal fees, and fewer workers' compensation claims.

Example: A large manufacturing company implemented CAPS and measured its success by tracking a 50% reduction in workplace harassment incidents over two years. The company also saw a 15% improvement in employee engagement scores, demonstrating that CAPS had a positive impact on both safety and morale.

Step 7: Sustaining Long-Term Success

For CAPS to have a lasting impact, organizations must commit to maintaining the system over the long term. This requires ongoing investment in training, technology, and resources, as well as a continued focus on prevention and early intervention.

Strategies for Sustaining Success:

- **Leadership Engagement**: Keep leadership actively involved in promoting CAPS and celebrating its successes. Regularly update leadership on the system's impact and the value it brings to the organization.

- **Evolving with the Organization**: As the organization grows or changes, CAPS must evolve as well. Ensure that the system is flexible enough to adapt to new challenges, such as remote work, global expansion, or changes in workplace dynamics.

- **Cultural Integration**: Embed CAPS into the organization's culture by making it a core part of safety and well being initiatives. When CAPS becomes second nature to staff and leadership, its impact will be sustained for the long term.

Example: At a global nonprofit organization, CAPS became a central part of the organization's culture, with leadership regularly showcasing CAPS data and success stories in company-wide meetings. This commitment to CAPS ensured that the system remained a priority and continued to deliver positive outcomes over time.

Conclusion: Ensuring Long-Term Success with CAPS

Successfully implementing CAPS requires more than just installing a system—it requires a commitment to fostering a culture of prevention, safety, and respect. By following these steps—securing leadership commitment, building a dedicated implementation team, providing comprehensive training, integrating with existing systems, and measuring success—organizations can ensure that CAPS is a long-term solution for preventing aggression and promoting well-being.

In the final chapter, we will summarize the key takeaways from this book and provide actionable insights for organizations looking to create safer, more productive environments through the implementation of CAPS.

Chapter 20

Culmination – CAPS: A Comprehensive System for a Safer Future

Throughout the preceding chapters, we've explored various aspects of aggression prevention, the limitations of existing systems, and the practical applications of the Critical Aggression Prevention System (CAPS). Now, we bring together all the elements that have been discussed and illustrate how CAPS operates as a comprehensive, evidence-based solution designed to identify and prevent aggression before it escalates into violence.

A System Built on Scientifically Reliable Measures

At the heart of CAPS is its ability to measure aggression with scientific reliability, distinguishing it from other systems that rely on subjective emotions like anger. As we've discussed, anger is personal and subjective—difficult to measure, and therefore difficult to manage. Aggression, however, manifests through observable behaviors and body language that can be scientifically quantified. CAPS enables first observers to detect these early warning signs, log them into the system, and provide real-time data that helps decision-makers intervene before an incident occurs.

This measurable approach means CAPS is not just another reactive system; it offers a proactive way to prevent violence. Using the aggression continuum, CAPS identifies escalating stages of aggression, allowing for early and targeted interventions. As discussed, aggression can be addressed before reaching that critical "moment of commitment," preventing harm while still preserving the dignity and well-being of the individual involved.

The CAPS Mobile App, Dashboard, and Learning Management System

Three key technological components make CAPS both powerful and easy to implement: the **CAPS Mobile App**, **CAPS Dashboard**, and **CAPS Learning Management System (LMS)**.

1. **CAPS Mobile App**: First observers—whether they are bus drivers, teachers, coaches, or security personnel—can use the CAPS Mobile App to log real-time observations of behaviors that indicate early stages of aggression. With a simple, user-friendly interface, the app allows first observers to document observable behaviors like withdrawn body language, clenched fists, or heightened agitation. This immediate input of data provides the foundation for the broader system's analysis.

2. **CAPS Dashboard**: Once the data is entered, the CAPS Dashboard aggregates the reports from various first observers into a single, color-coded platform. This color-coding makes it easy for administrators to assess the totality of circumstances at a glance. For example, if one observer logs a student at Stage 3 (withdrawal), and another reports the same student escalating to Stage 4 (hostility), administrators can quickly see the trend and intervene before the aggression reaches Stage 5 (physical aggression). The dashboard provides a real-time, comprehensive view, allowing decision-makers to respond efficiently and with precision.

3. **CAPS Learning Management System (LMS)**: The CAPS LMS offers online training modules that ensure every individual involved with the system understands how to identify and report aggressive behaviors. This training is critical, as it equips all staff members—whether in schools, workplaces, or other settings—with the tools they need to be effective first observers. The training is scalable and self-paced, making it easy to implement across a wide variety of organizations without disrupting daily operations.

Why "See Something, Say Something" Falls Short

One of the key challenges with existing safety initiatives like "See Something, Say Something" is that they rely on people reporting behaviors out of altruism or fear. But as we've discussed, people naturally act in their own self-interest. They may hesitate to report something they see because they fear retribution or because they don't want to cause harm to the individual they're reporting. Current systems are reactive and often punitive, punishing those who are identified as offenders of bullying or aggression, which discourages people from getting involved.

With CAPS, the system flips this dynamic on its head. Instead of waiting for aggressive behaviors to escalate into punishable offenses, CAPS identifies precursors to aggression and intervenes early. The goal is not to punish but to rehabilitate. This proactive approach reassures first observers that the person they are reporting on will be helped rather than harmed, making them far more likely to report what they see. In fact, many individuals who have been intervened upon through CAPS end up thanking those who reported them, recognizing that early intervention saved them from more severe consequences.

The Role of First Observers: Detecting the Path to Violence

A fundamental aspect of CAPS is its ability to track aggression as it escalates through various stages. For example, a bus operator may observe a student at Stage 3—withdrawn and isolated. A teacher may later notice that the same student displaying hostile behavior (Stage 4). By the time a coach sees the student physically pushing another (Stage 5), CAPS has logged all of these reports, creating a clear trend. This pattern shows that the student is on the path to violence, creating a sense of urgency to intervene and diffuse the situation before it escalates further.

Does this mean the individual is guaranteed to be violent? Not necessarily. But what it does mean is that administrators now have a window of opportunity to step in and engage before an incident occurs. By understanding the progression of aggression, CAPS allows staff to engage in a timely, effective way, addressing the underlying causes of the behavior and preventing an incident from materializing.

CAPS in Action: A Case Study

Let's consider an example of how CAPS operates in a school setting, combining all of these elements. A bus driver notices a student acting unusually withdrawn in the morning and logs this behavior into the CAPS Mobile App. Later, a teacher observes the same student displaying signs of hostility, such as clenched fists and mumbling under their breath. The gym coach notices the student pushing a peer during class. Each of these observations is logged into the CAPS system, and the CAPS Dashboard shows a clear pattern of escalation. Administrators can now see the totality of the circumstances and respond accordingly.

Rather than waiting for the aggression to reach a crisis point, the school counselor intervenes early. A conversation with the student reveals that they've been experiencing bullying and had planned to retaliate. By intervening early, the school not only prevents an act of violence but also helps the student find a positive way forward, addressing the root of their aggression.

The Highest Form of Evidence-Based Best Practices

An administrator using the CAPS Dashboard gains immediate visibility into potential risks across their facility. The system's color-coded alerts provide a clear, visual representation of aggression levels, allowing administrators to quickly assess the totality of circumstances and respond efficiently and effectively. CAPS provides an actionable, data-driven approach that not only ensures the highest standards of safety but also supports early intervention. By identifying risks proactively through scientifically reliable methods, administrators can make informed decisions to create an environment where people feel supported, behaviors are understood, and potential incidents are diffused before they escalate. This enables organizations to implement the best evidence-based practices for aggression prevention, focusing not just on violence prevention but on fostering a culture of safety and trust.

Conclusion: CAPS as the Future of Aggression Prevention

The Critical Aggression Prevention System is a culmination of decades of research, practical application, and scientific reliability. It is designed to fill the gaps where other systems fall short, offering a preventive, rehabilitative, and evidence-based approach to aggression management. By bringing all these elements together—mobile technology, real-time dashboards, and comprehensive training—CAPS equips organizations with the tools they need to create safer schools, workplaces, and communities.

As we conclude this book, remember that CAPS is more than just a system; it's a commitment to fostering environments where people feel safe, supported, and empowered. It is my hope that with the implementation of CAPS, we can collectively move from reacting to violence to preventing it, ensuring a safer future for all.

The Path Forward: Scaling CAPS Across Diverse Environments

While CAPS is highly effective in schools, its framework is versatile and adaptable to a variety of environments—workplaces, public spaces, healthcare facilities, and beyond. The universality of aggression indicators means the system can be applied wherever there is human interaction, ensuring that safety measures are both proactive and scalable.

For organizations, implementing CAPS offers a significant return on investment. By preventing incidents before they occur, institutions save on the costs associated with violence, such as medical expenses, legal liabilities, damaged reputations, and lost productivity. In schools, this means fewer suspensions, improved student outcomes, and a safer learning environment. In workplaces, it means fewer workplace disruptions, reduced turnover, and increased employee morale.

CAPS Beyond Schools: A Broader Application for Society

Consider a healthcare setting, where aggression is not uncommon—whether from stressed patients, overwhelmed family members, or frustrated staff. By training hospital employees to observe aggression precursors, logging observations into the CAPS Mobile App, and using the CAPS Dashboard to monitor trends, administrators can intervene before situations escalate to violence. Just as in schools, the system fosters early intervention, turning potentially volatile situations into manageable conversations, where individuals are guided toward de-escalation rather than disciplinary action or physical restraint.

In retail environments, where customer service representatives and security personnel often face aggressive behaviors, the application of

CAPS can prevent workplace violence. Training employees to recognize early aggression indicators empowers them to take appropriate action before tensions boil over, ensuring that both customers and staff are protected.

Public safety organizations—like the Secret Service, as I have advocated in previous outreach—are ideal candidates for the CAPS framework. CAPS could serve as a reliable tool for identifying individuals on the path to violence, supplementing existing methods with scientific reliability and technology that offers a more efficient, data-driven approach.

A Rehabilitative Approach: CAPS as a Transformative Tool

As we've discussed, the CAPS system is not designed to punish or label individuals as offenders. Instead, it operates as a rehabilitative tool that gives individuals the opportunity to be redirected before they cause harm. This is a fundamental shift from the current punitive models, which often leave individuals feeling cornered, stigmatized, or retaliatory.

By identifying aggression before it escalates, CAPS offers the chance to change someone's trajectory. The system's rehabilitative focus allows for interventions that guide individuals toward constructive alternatives, helping them work through underlying frustrations or stresses before they manifest in aggressive behavior. This approach fosters a culture of understanding and support, making people more likely to report concerning behavior, knowing that they are helping rather than punishing the individual.

Why CAPS Is the Solution for Today and Tomorrow

We live in an era where aggression—both verbal and physical—seems to be on the rise, from schools to workplaces to public spaces. Traditional methods that react after the fact are not enough. We need a system that not only identifies the earliest warning signs but also gives us the tools to intervene effectively. CAPS fills this critical gap, offering a scientifically reliable, proactive approach that has been proven to work in real-world environments.

CAPS is also future-proof. As aggression continues to evolve, the system's foundation in measurable, evidence-based practices ensures it will remain relevant and adaptable. New technologies can be integrated into the platform, and additional training modules can be developed to address emerging challenges, whether they involve cyberbullying, workplace harassment, or public safety threats.

Final Thoughts: A Safer Future Starts Here

As we conclude this journey, it is important to recognize the unique value of CAPS as both a preventive and rehabilitative tool. It offers a path forward for schools, workplaces, and society at large—a path that prioritizes safety, understanding, and early intervention. With CAPS, we are not just reacting to violence; we are preventing it, one observation, one intervention, and one life at a time.

The adoption of CAPS represents a paradigm shift in how we manage aggression. Instead of waiting for incidents to occur and then picking up the pieces, we now have the power to stop them before they happen. This is the promise of CAPS, and it is my hope that through the lessons and insights shared in this book, you will join me in embracing this proactive approach to create a safer future for all.

Let us take the first step together, ensuring that every school, workplace, and community is equipped with the tools necessary to protect those who matter most—our children, our families, our colleagues, and our communities.

The Future of CAPS: Expanding Its Reach

As we look toward the future, it's essential to consider the broader implications of CAPS and how it can be expanded to serve an even wider range of environments and needs. While the system is already proving effective in schools, workplaces, and public safety organizations, its potential goes far beyond these settings. The adaptability of the CAPS framework allows for its integration into virtually any space where people gather, interact, and sometimes, conflict.

Schools as the Foundation

Schools will always be a focal point for CAPS, given the unique vulnerabilities of young people. Children and teens are in the most formative stages of their lives, and the environments we create for them have long-lasting effects on their development. By embedding CAPS into school culture, we're not only making campuses safer but also teaching future generations the value of early intervention, emotional regulation, and non-violent conflict resolution. These lessons extend far beyond school walls; they become life skills that students carry into adulthood, helping them navigate challenges at universities, workplaces, and personal relationships.

When students enter college or the workforce, they carry the tools provided by systems like CAPS with them. Early exposure to a culture of prevention and support helps students recognize and manage their own aggressive tendencies and respond to aggression in others in a more constructive way. In this sense, CAPS is more than a system—it's a transformative tool for shaping the next generation of leaders, innovators, and citizens.

A Universal Tool for Aggression Management

The CAPS system isn't limited by geography, culture, or organizational structure. Whether implemented in a small business, a multinational corporation, or a university campus, its principles remain the same: early identification, reliable data, and a focus on prevention and rehabilitation. In any setting, CAPS helps foster a culture of trust and safety where aggression is addressed before it spirals into violence.

Consider how CAPS could be used in large public gatherings—sporting events, concerts, or even protests. By training security teams and staff to recognize early aggression indicators and equipping them with the CAPS Mobile App and Dashboard, event organizers can prevent violence in highly charged environments. Imagine a scenario where an aggressive fan is noticed displaying signs of escalation in a stadium; by logging that behavior early, security can intervene and diffuse the situation, keeping both the individual and others safe.

In healthcare settings, CAPS can be a lifesaving tool for preventing aggression toward staff. Hospitals and clinics, where stress and emotions often run high, are prime environments for aggression to surface. By implementing CAPS, healthcare administrators can better protect their staff, reduce workplace violence, and maintain an environment of care and respect.

CAPS as a Global Standard

The versatility and scientific foundation of CAPS make it ideal for adoption as a global standard for aggression management. As aggression and violence continue to challenge societies worldwide, CAPS offers a unified, reliable approach that transcends borders. In regions experiencing high levels of violence or unrest, CAPS can serve as a vital tool for restoring peace and order through early intervention. Governments, NGOs, and international organizations could all benefit from a system like CAPS that is scientifically validated and scalable across different cultural contexts.

Technology-Driven Prevention: The Next Frontier

As technology evolves, so too will CAPS. The future of the system lies in its ability to harness new technologies to make aggression management even more precise and effective. Artificial intelligence and machine learning, for example, could be integrated into the CAPS Dashboard to enhance the system's ability to detect patterns of aggression. Predictive analytics could help identify not only individuals who may be on the path to violence but also broader trends that indicate rising tensions in a community or organization.

Additionally, the ongoing development of mobile technology will make CAPS even more accessible. Imagine a future where students, employees, and the general public can participate in aggression prevention by using apps that connect directly to the CAPS Dashboard. This would create a network of first observers far broader than ever before, empowering entire communities to take part in keeping each other safe.

A Call to Action

As we bring this book to a close, it is crucial to remember that the success of CAPS relies on its widespread adoption and the commitment of individuals and organizations to embrace a preventive, rather than reactive, approach to aggression. The system is in place, the tools are available, and the science is clear: CAPS works. But it needs champions—those willing to stand up and advocate for a safer, more compassionate world.

Whether you are an educator, a business leader, a healthcare professional, or a concerned citizen, you have the power to make a difference. By implementing CAPS in your environment, you are taking a bold step toward creating spaces where people feel safe, valued, and supported. You are contributing to a culture where aggression is addressed early, where individuals are rehabilitated rather than punished, and where violence is not just responded to, but prevented.

Thank you for taking this journey with me. Together, we can transform the way the world manages aggression, ensuring that future generations inherit a safer, more peaceful society. CAPS is not just a system—it's a movement. And that movement begins with you.

Sustaining CAPS: Ensuring Long-Term Success

As we look to the future, sustaining the impact of CAPS will require a commitment not only to the initial implementation but also to the continuous improvement of the system. The effectiveness of CAPS lies in its adaptability, and to ensure its long-term success, organizations must remain engaged with the latest advancements in both technology and human behavior research.

Continuous Learning and Development

To maintain CAPS' effectiveness, regular training and development are essential. CAPS' Learning Management System (LMS) should evolve alongside the challenges of modern-day aggression, providing first observers with up-to-date tools and strategies. Ongoing education will ensure that the system remains responsive to emerging threats, including new forms of aggression that may arise in the digital age, such as cyberbullying or online harassment.

Organizations that adopt CAPS should schedule periodic refresher courses for their teams. Just as physical safety protocols require regular drills and updates, CAPS relies on continuous engagement from all involved. The more familiar observers become with aggression indicators and reporting processes, the quicker and more efficiently they can respond.

Data-Driven Evolution

One of CAPS' strongest assets is its ability to gather and analyze data in real time. Over time, as organizations accumulate more data through the CAPS Dashboard, trends and patterns will emerge that can help refine and improve the system. Organizations must commit to regularly reviewing their CAPS data, not just to prevent immediate incidents but also to gain insights that can inform future safety strategies.

By leveraging this data, organizations can spot long-term trends, such as which areas or individuals may require additional support and make data-driven decisions about resource allocation and policy changes. The CAPS system isn't static; it's dynamic, designed to grow stronger as more data is gathered.

Expanding the Reach of CAPS

To maximize its impact, CAPS must be adopted on a broader scale, reaching not only schools and workplaces but entire communities. Engaging with local governments, law enforcement agencies, and community organizations could help bring the benefits of CAPS to public spaces, events, and other environments where aggression may arise. The goal is to make CAPS not just a system used by institutions but a standard for aggression management that is embraced by society at large.

Advocates for CAPS should work to establish partnerships with government agencies, educational institutions, and private sector leaders, showing how CAPS can be adapted to a variety of environments. By demonstrating its scalability and flexibility, CAPS can become a go-to solution for aggression prevention on a national or even global scale.

CAPS as a Model for Global Adoption

There is no reason that CAPS should be limited by borders. Aggression is a universal human challenge, and the principles behind CAPS—early detection, scientific reliability, and prevention—are applicable worldwide. Countries facing high levels of violence or conflict could benefit immensely from adopting CAPS as part of their national safety strategy.

Governments and international organizations could implement CAPS on a larger scale, using its data-driven approach to address systemic aggression issues in a coordinated, proactive manner. Just as CAPS can be scaled down to individual schools or businesses, it can also be scaled up to address national security, public safety, and social cohesion.

Chapter 20

Final Words: Empowering Safe Schools and Safer Futures, Coming Full Circle

As we bring this book to its conclusion, I want to leave you with a sense of hope. Aggression may be an age-old human challenge, but with CAPS, we have a tool that can change the way we approach it. CAPS empowers individuals and organizations to take control of their environments, to recognize the early signs of aggression, and to intervene before harm occurs. It shifts the paradigm from reaction to prevention, from punishment to rehabilitation, and from fear to action.

The system itself is only as strong as the people who use it. Each of us has a role to play in creating a safer future, whether by implementing CAPS in our schools, businesses, or communities, or by simply learning to recognize the early signs of aggression and speaking up. Together, we can build a world where aggression is no longer ignored, but addressed—early, effectively, and with compassion.

Thank you for joining me on this journey. The future is ours to shape, and with CAPS, we have the tools to make it safer and more secure for everyone.

SAFER SCHOOLS/SAFER FUTURE: By creating safer schools today for our children, grandchildren, and, in my case, great-grandchildren, we are not only protecting their future but also fostering a more trusting and resilient community—locally, nationally, and globally. Together, we can build a world where safety and trust are the foundation for a better tomorrow.

NOTE:

Interested in Mastering Aggression Prevention?

If you're looking to gain comprehensive training in identifying and preventing aggression, consider enrolling in our **Aggression First Observers' Online Course** and **Certified Aggression Managers' Online Course**. These courses offer the knowledge and tools for early identification and prevention of aggression.

To get started, simply contact us:

- **Phone**: (407) 718-5637
- **Email**: info@AggressionManagement.com

Upon completion of the Certified Aggression Managers' Course, you'll receive a **Certificate of Completion** from the Center for Aggression Management, Inc.

Chapter 21

THE ANATOMY OF A SCHOOL SHOOTER

Only when we can measure something can we truly manage it. This principle holds true in many realms of life, but particularly for aggressive behavior, which can quickly escalate when left unchecked, especially in school-aged students. At the core of understanding and managing aggressive behavior are the Primal and Cognitive Aggression Continua.

To begin with, it's essential to distinguish between **assertive** and **aggressive behavior**. Assertive behavior involves expressing oneself confidently and respectfully with the intent to be mutually beneficial and without the intent to harm others. It's rooted in self-assurance and constructive communication, aiming to manage aggressive behavior while respecting the boundaries of others. Aggressive behavior, by contrast, is marked by a disregard for these boundaries, often fueled by intense emotions and/or a desire to control or dominate others. While assertive actions are essential for positive self-expression and managing aggression, this aggression crosses into harmful territory, where intent to harm, escalation, and the potential for violence can take hold.

- The **Primal Aggression Continuum** measures adrenaline-driven responses to external triggers, such as anger, frustration, and rage. These natural but impulsive reactions are common in teenagers, often stemming from emotional stressors such as social pressure, academic stress, or personal struggles. They are both instinctive and emotionally driven.
- The **Cognitive Aggression Continuum,** on the other hand, examines the escalation of deliberate, intent-driven behavior, characterized by the conscious planning and directing of harm toward others. For students, this could manifest as bullying, physical confrontation, or other forms of calculated aggression such as cyberbullying and/or creating hostile environments.

Understanding both continua offers critical insight into the nature and severity of displayed aggression. It helps us spot the early warning signs, or precursors, of violence. While many of these apparently benign indicators, such as emotional outbursts, withdrawal from friends, or lingering resentment might seem harmless at first, we know from research that they can, and often do, metastasize into significantly more malicious behaviors if left unaddressed.

THE STORY OF JAMES DOUGLAS

James Douglas, or "Jimmy" to those who know him, is a 16-year-old junior at Worthington High School. As his neighbor and teammate, you've been close friends with him for the past decade. Jimmy is a familiar face at school—quiet, friendly, and easygoing. He's a good student, plays football, and is polite to both teachers and classmates. Though not the loudest or most popular, he's dependable, and people get along well with him. Teachers appreciate his respectfulness, and friends enjoy his company, whether on a weekend hunting trip or playing video games. Despite his friendly nature, however, there's a bit of mystery to Jimmy. He's assertive in a subtle, non-confrontational way, keeping a steady presence but generally keeping to himself. His easygoing but reserved nature makes him approachable, while still keeping him at a comfortable distance from others.

TRIGGER PHASE

When individuals effectively cope with daily stresses—those triggers we all encounter—they maintain a calm, stable demeanor, demonstrating resilience. In this balanced state, we say everything is "copasetic." However, when coping skills begin to falter, we see a shift in behavior and communication. This is where our Primal and Cognitive Aggression Continua come into play.

On the Primal side of the Aggression Continuum, when coping mechanisms begin to break down, individuals respond instinctively with adrenaline-driven reactions, signaling their entry into Stage One, or "Mounting Anxiety." At this stage, their behavior becomes visibly affected: thinking may appear scattered or disjointed, posture turns tense, and tone shifts abruptly. These physical and verbal indicators reflect a struggle to retain emotional control, fueled by heightened adrenaline. As individuals progress along this Primal Aggression Continuum, their quality of judgment declines, making it crucial to engage, diffuse, and redirect early. Doing so not only prevents further escalation but also makes it easier to guide them back on course and away from this path of aggression.

In contrast, on the Cognitive side of the continuum, the Trigger Phase is more calculated. Here, assertive behavior—which is typically cooperative, caring, and mutually beneficial—begins to shift subtly. This stage often starts with assertive self-expression but can devolve into dominant or even hostile actions as the individual begins to exert control, often marked by individuals who feel they must control all of the people around them. Instead of instinctive reactions, these behaviors are intent-driven, revealing a shift from cooperation to dominance.

By recognizing these early signs on both the Primal and Cognitive Continua, we can intervene before aggression takes root and escalates. These shifts mark the critical transition from the Coping Trigger Phase to Stage One, signaling a change that, if left unchecked, may intensify over time.

STAGE 1: THE ESCALATION PHASE AND NOT COPING

Usually, Jimmy was the steady one—the friend everyone could count on to keep his cool, no matter what the situation. But today was different. The trouble had started early, snowballing from a rough morning into an even rougher day. Jimmy had stayed up late the night before, cramming for a test he knew he wasn't ready for. By the time he finally went to bed, sleep was hard to come by. His mind had raced with formulas and facts that refused to stick.

When his alarm finally blared, he felt like he had barely closed his eyes. In the scramble that followed, he hit snooze one too many times, jolting awake with barely enough time to throw on clothes and rush through his morning routine. Breakfast was out of the question; he grabbed his backpack and dashed out the door, only to watch his bus pulling away. Heart pounding, he caught up just in time, but his nerves were already shot. He took his seat, disheveled and groggy, as the bus rolled towards school.

Chapter 21

By the time he made it to homeroom, Jimmy's patience was wearing thin. He kept his head down, hoping to get through the morning without incident. But it wasn't long before a classmate made an offhand remark—something about the test Jimmy had stayed up for. Normally, he'd brush it off with a shrug or a joke, but today was different. He snapped back, his tone sharp and uncharacteristically biting, leaving the other student taken aback. As the minutes dragged on, Jimmy found himself brooding over the exchange, replaying it in his mind as if it were some great injustice. He knew it was small, yet he couldn't shake it. The weight of the day seemed to press down on him, each annoyance magnified.

When lunch finally came, Jimmy felt his tension reaching a breaking point. He joined his friends, hoping to distract himself, but his frustration clung to him. He picked at his food, barely listening as his friends talked and laughed. When his best friend nudged him, trying to get a reaction, Jimmy snapped—his words harsh, cold, and out of character. Silence fell over the group as his friend stared, startled and hurt, but Jimmy couldn't bring himself to apologize. Instead, he pushed back his chair and walked away, leaving them in stunned silence.

Alone in the crowded hallway, Jimmy's heart raced as he tried to regain his composure. The calm, steady Jimmy everyone relied on felt like a stranger today, unraveling under the weight of his own frayed nerves. The anger and frustration simmered within him, and each attempt to steady himself only seemed to fan the flames. Every noise, every glance from a passing student felt amplified, reminding him of how close he was to losing control. He took a shaky breath and braced himself, hoping he could hold it together, but feeling more uncertain with every step.

COMMENTARY

Jimmy was stepping onto the first rung of the aggression continuum, a precarious threshold where primal frustration and cognitive discontent began to blur the lines he usually held firm. His triggers had been stacking up—running late for school, feeling unprepared for an upcoming test, and ongoing tension with classmates—and now, something within him had shifted, creating a perfect storm of emotional turmoil.

At first, the signs of his struggle seemed innocent, almost imperceptible to the untrained eye. You began to notice small changes in him: his usual relaxed demeanor was replaced by a quiet tension that was hard to place.

He seemed quieter than usual, his eyes lacking the familiar spark that once animated his conversations. His presence felt distant and distracted, as though he were physically present but mentally adrift. When you approached him to ask if something was wrong, he muttered vaguely, "Just a rough morning," while avoiding your gaze. It seemed that Jimmy was not telling the truth. There was a tone in his voice that felt off—tinged with an uncharacteristic edge—but you brushed it aside, attributing it to the stress of school. It seemed subtle—easy to dismiss as just a bad day.

However, for those trained to spot early signs of escalating aggression—like Aggression First Observers or Certified Aggression Managers—these moments matter significantly. **Stage 1 represents the optimal opportunity for trained CAPS personnel to intervene,** even without knowing the specific details of Jimmy's morning. They understand that such seemingly minor shifts in behavior can signal deeper, more concerning issues. With their expertise, they know the right questions to ask, creating an environment where Jimmy might feel safe enough to express what he's going through.

They are adept at recognizing patterns: the way his laughter doesn't quite reach his eyes anymore, the subtle fidgeting of his hands, and the occasional scowl that flashes across his face like a micro-expression during moments of stress. Each sign is a piece of a larger puzzle that, if left unaddressed, could lead to serious consequences. Yes, it's crucial for trained observers to act before the aggression continuum escalates beyond a point of no return, but well before this becomes a Stage 4 "incident" of sexual harassment, abuse, bullying, discrimination and/or violent behavior. They might approach Jimmy in a genuine and caring way initiating a casual conversation, asking Jimmy how he's coping with school pressures or if he wants to talk about what might be bothering him today.

Their ability to engage Jimmy at this early stage could be the best opportunity to redirect his path, offering him the support he needs to navigate his frustrations in a healthier way. By fostering a sense of trust and open communication, they can help him regain a sense of control over his emotions before they spiral into something more dangerous. Recognizing the importance of this early intervention, CAPS personnel understand that timely action can make all the difference in preventing an escalation of aggression and ensuring that students like Jimmy receive the guidance they need to address their challenges constructively.

Chapter 21

> **Note:** As one progresses on the aggression continuum, judgment declines. The earlier we intervene to diffuse and redirect, the easier it is to guide someone like Jimmy away from the path toward escalating aggression.

STAGE 2: NEGATIVE BIAS AND FIXATION

Later that day, you talk to Jimmy again. As his friend and confidant, he opens up to you in ways he wouldn't with others. The conversation starts light, but when you bring up the upcoming hunting trip, something in Jimmy shifts. He begins venting about an incident where another student got him in trouble with a teacher. "She just doesn't get it," he says, frustration simmering beneath his words. "Thinks she knows everything. People like that don't deserve respect."

What started as simple frustration has deepened into something more unsettling, he is becoming fixated. Jimmy's irritation isn't just about that one incident—it feels personal now, and he doesn't seem to take any responsibility for his role in this grievance. His anger has grown into a simmering resentment, and he speaks as though he's been wronged. A rough day has now become a lingering bitterness. When others speak well of her, he blows them off, as if he did not hear them.

As Jimmy keeps talking, you notice something troubling. He's no longer venting about general stressors—he's fixated on this one incident and the student he blames for it. His resentment clouds his perspective. "She doesn't deserve to be in the same class as me," he mutters under his breath, his voice tightening. There's a sharpness in his tone, and you can feel the weight of his emotions. What started as a small grievance has transformed into a grudge.

Jimmy begins consuming media that seems to reinforce his anger. The "us vs. them" mentality becomes part of his worldview, and you learn that you don't trust "them." This deepens his fixation. He starts to internalize messages from social media and online forums, seeing the world in stark divisions. His classmate comes to represent everything wrong in his life, fueling his frustrations and blurring his judgment.

What's most concerning is Jimmy's shift in accountability. He starts blaming others for his problems, particularly this student, rather than considering his own role in the conflict. His empathy fades, and casual debates with friends turn into heated arguments driven by a sense of moral superiority. Jimmy believes he alone sees the truth, drawing further away from those who once felt close to him.

COMMENTARY

Stage 2 is a crucial juncture where Aggression First Observers and Certified Aggression Managers can effectively intervene. At this stage, Jimmy has moved beyond typical expressions of frustration and entered a more serious realm of aggression, manifesting itself along both the Primal (adrenaline-driven) and Cognitive (intent-driven) Aggression Continua. On the Primal side, his emotions—anger, frustration, and a pervasive sense of being wronged—continue to fuel his mindset. However, on the Cognitive side, his thinking is becoming increasingly distorted; he is no longer viewing his peer with a balanced perspective but is beginning to perceive her as a problem that needs solving, setting the stage for a troubling escalation.

As Jimmy moves along the Primal Aggression Continuum, he begins losing trust in those he would typically rely on. Influenced by certain blogs, podcasts, and media outlets, he's told repeatedly that those around him are not to be trusted; they're part of "them," not "us." This growing divide is steering him closer to more dangerous forms of aggression. His primal, adrenaline-fueled anxiety, combined with a cognitive fixation on perceived injustices, fuels his emotional turbulence, making him increasingly agitated. Jimmy now starts to frame his frustrations not as fleeting emotions but as a personal vendetta, reinforcing a belief that the world is fundamentally biased against him. This skewed perception is alarming, as it propels him further along the Aggression Continua, where primal instincts meet calculated thoughts of retribution, intensifying his descent into aggression.

Without the oversight of a Critical Aggression Prevention System (CAPS), these critical warning signs may go unnoticed. The signs of Jimmy's deteriorating emotional and mental state are often subtle, easily dismissed by peers and adults alike as typical teenage angst. Yet, this lack of recognition can have devastating consequences. Left unchecked, Jimmy's fixation on his perceived injustices, coupled with his growing resentment, could propel him toward aggressive actions. He may start to see harm as a valid response to the grievances he believes he's endured, constructing a dangerous narrative that could ultimately lead to violence. These thoughts aren't directed aggressively or violently toward any specific person but are more a justification of harm as retribution against an undefined antagonist.

As Jimmy's emotional landscape grows darker, his cognitive processes become more rigid, making it increasingly difficult for him to see alternative perspectives or solutions. He might dismiss advice from friends or authority figures, convinced that only he understands the gravity of his situation. The notion of empathy, which once guided his interactions, begins to fade, replaced by a singular focus on rectifying what he perceives as wrongs. This shift not only isolates him from his support system but also intensifies the risk of escalation.

Intervention at this stage is essential. A Certified Aggression Manager would be trained to recognize the signs of this dangerous transformation, identifying key indicators such as Jimmy's increasingly hostile thoughts and emotional outbursts. By engaging with Jimmy in a constructive manner, they could help him process his feelings and reframe his understanding of the conflict with his peer. Such an intervention might involve facilitating open dialogue between Jimmy and the student he feels wronged by, allowing for reconciliation and restoring a sense of agency in a healthier, more constructive way.

Ultimately, Stage 2 serves as a pivotal opportunity for intervention, highlighting the critical need for proactive measures within educational environments. By equipping educators and peers with the tools to recognize the signs of escalating aggression, the CAPS framework aims to create a culture of awareness and support. This preventative approach not only addresses individual cases like Jimmy's but also fosters a more compassionate and resilient community, where students feel empowered to seek help and where conflicts can be resolved before they escalate into crises.

STAGE 3: INDEPENDENT AND DEFIANT

Days go by, and Jimmy's behavior shifts in ways that are hard to ignore. Once a cooperative classmate, he now isolates himself, refusing to collaborate. During class discussions, he disregards his teachers' instructions, preferring to work alone. When classmates try to engage him, he brushes them off with short, impatient replies. His isolation is becoming obvious, but teachers know Jimmy as a good kid, and chalk it up to typical teenage moodiness, assuming he'll snap out of it eventually.

But this time, it's different.

Jimmy's frustration over an incident where a classmate got him in trouble with a teacher has only deepened.

It's clear that Jimmy continues to detach from her and is becoming self-absorbed in his defiance of her.

He has not stopped discussing anxiety, he will now expresses views through his actions not through his words (e.g. hate websites or blogs). Each step of this continuum, he loses more of his quality of judgement.

"She doesn't deserve to be in the same class as me," he mutters, his voice tight with emotion. There's a hard edge to his words, and you can feel the intensity of his feelings. What began as a minor incident has hardened into a lasting grudge.

COMMENTARY

While teachers and friends notice that Jimmy's behavior has changed, they remember that Jimmy is "a good kid" and dismiss it as a typical phase of adolescence, hoping that he will eventually return to his usual self. Part of the problem here is that the adults around Jimmy are captivated by the impression of Jimmy as "a good kid" and find it difficult to fathom him as an "aggressor." They attribute his withdrawal, irritability, and dark humor to teenage angst, failing to grasp the depth of his internal turmoil. What they don't realize, however, is that Jimmy is slipping into a deeper, more entrenched state of aggression, which Aggression First Observers and Certified Aggression Managers are trained to see. His rationality and judgment are deteriorating, creating a dangerous disconnect between how he perceives himself and how he is affecting those around him. He doesn't see himself as an aggressor; instead, he believes he is justified in his feelings, convinced that his actions are merely a response to the injustices he perceives.

This seething anger and cold detachment, however, have profound effects on those around him—his supposed "perpetrator," as well as his family, friends, and teachers. His relationships grow strained as his isolation deepens, leaving him more vulnerable to his destructive thoughts. Friends who once enjoyed his company find themselves bewildered by his increasingly erratic behavior, while teachers express concern but feel ill-equipped to intervene effectively. The lack of understanding and connection exacerbates his sense of alienation, pushing him further into his own world of resentment and vengeance, which is easy to find on aligned blogs, podcasts and websites.

Had a Critical Aggression Prevention System (CAPS) been in place, these troubling shifts in Jimmy's behavior could have been detected much earlier. Aggression First Observers, and Certified Aggression Managers are trained to identify signs of escalating aggression. They would have recognized that Jimmy's frustration had morphed into something far more serious. One or more Certified Aggression Managers could have initiated a dialogue with Jimmy, perhaps even coordinating a meeting with the involved parties—his classmate and the teachers—to address the underlying issues directly. Such intervention could have provided Jimmy with a constructive outlet for his feelings, helping him understand that this conflict does not have to define his identity or dictate his actions.

Instead, without such support, Jimmy's aggression continues to spiral, leading him down a path of isolation and defiance. His cold detachment alienates him further from his peers, reinforcing the very narratives of betrayal and victimization he clings to. The absence of intervention not only leaves Jimmy trapped in his destructive mindset but also allows the situation to escalate unchecked, ultimately heightening the risk of violence. Each missed opportunity for dialogue and understanding deepens his despair, pushing him closer to the edge where he feels he must take drastic action to reclaim his sense of power and control.

This progression highlights the essential role of early intervention and strong support systems within schools. By identifying signs of aggression early on, educators and Certified Aggression Managers can create an environment where students feel heard and valued, cultivating healthier relationships and preventing aggressive incidents before they develop. It's clear that there were multiple opportunities to diffuse and redirect Jimmy's path. Certified Aggression Managers are specifically trained not only to de-escalate aggression but to help the individual see the negative consequences of their current trajectory. They then guide the individual toward a more constructive path that addresses their concerns without severe repercussions. Through the coordinated efforts of Aggression First Observers and Certified Aggression Managers, institutions can actively prevent incidents of sexual harassment, abuse, bullying, discrimination, and even assault or violence, showcasing real-time evidence-based commitment to a safer, more supportive environment.

STAGE 4: COVERT AGGRESSION AND SPREADING DISCONTENT

A week later, a close friend of Jimmy's pulls you aside with a concerned expression. "Hey, have you seen what Jimmy posted on social media?" they ask, their voice low as they pull out their phone. They show you a cryptic message Jimmy put up the night before. The post is directed at the student he's been upset with, accusing her of being "fake" and suggesting that others shouldn't trust her. While it's not an outright threat, it's evident that Jimmy is trying to turn his peers against her, sowing seeds of discontent.

You can't help but feel a knot tighten in your stomach as you read his words. It feels unsettling, like a warning sign flashing in front of you. Some of Jimmy's classmates have noticed his behavior changing recently, but because he's well-liked and respected, they hesitate to speak up. They dismiss it as typical high school drama, not wanting to risk being labeled as "snitches." The fear of potential backlash looms large; without solid evidence to back up their concerns, they worry about the social fallout that could come from intervening.

Even the teachers, who see Jimmy as a good kid simply going through a rough patch, remain blissfully unaware of the growing aggression bubbling beneath the surface. They miss the signs that indicate his emotional state is deteriorating—his isolation, the sharpness in his tone, and now this veiled attack on social media. It's as if everyone around him is underestimating the seriousness of the situation, allowing Jimmy's bitterness and resentment to fester unchecked.

As one of Jimmy's best friends and confidents the days pass by, you find yourself caught in a moral dilemma. Should you bring this troubling behavior to someone's attention, or should you remain silent, hoping it will blow over and you don't want to lose Jimmy's friendship? You feel a growing responsibility to act, knowing that if no one intervenes, the damage could escalate beyond just words on a screen. The thought of Jimmy's anger spiraling out of control weighs heavily on your mind, and you realize that this isn't just about high school drama anymore—it's about the potential for real harm, both to Jimmy and to the student he's targeting.

Chapter 21

COMMENTARY

In Stage 4, Jimmy's aggression has evolved from mere frustration into something more calculated, marking a critical point of transition where more unseen aggressive personality traits shift into directed aggression toward specific individuals. This stage represents the debarkation from internalized frustration to covertly expressed aggression, setting the stage for the emergence of incidents such as bullying, abuse, sexual harassment, discrimination, and, potentially, more severe assaultive and violent behavior as the Aggression Continuum progresses.

While aggression in Stages 1, 2, and 3 typically flies below the radar and remains unseen by most, Stage 4 signals a shift. Though still covert, this is where harmful behaviors like bullying and harassment begin to surface and become more apparent to those around. The escalation from subtle, internalized frustration to more directed, visible actions increases the likelihood that these behaviors will be noticed, making Stage 4 a crucial point for intervention.

As discussed in the book, when it comes to aggressive incidents, current programs typically focus on identifying and punishing offenders, creating a punitive atmosphere. This approach often deters students from reporting incidents, as they seek to avoid the drama and conflict that follow, leaving concerning behavior unreported. This is why "See Something Say Something" is not reliable. In contrast, CAPS (Critical Aggression Prevention System) offers a rehabilitative approach, empowering students to see themselves as part of the solution. By fostering a proactive mindset, CAPS helps prevent negative outcomes for individuals like Jimmy by encouraging students to voice their concerns within a supportive environment.

Without CAPS in place, Jimmy's escalating behavior could easily go unnoticed, precisely when intervention is most crucial. A Certified Aggression Manager would be trained to recognize that Jimmy's actions are no longer just expressions of frustration but deliberate attempts to harm his peer's reputation. Early intervention could facilitate a constructive conversation between Jimmy and the affected student, defusing tensions before they escalate into something more harmful.

Moreover, CAPS utilizes objective, measurable, human-based precursor behaviors that do not infringe upon HIPAA, FERPA, or the Civil Rights

Act of 1964. This makes it easier for teachers, acting as Aggression First Observers, to recognize and report these concerning behaviors without fear of breaching privacy or civil rights regulations. This structured, objective approach cultivates a culture of awareness and accountability, establishing a safer environment for everyone involved.

STAGE 5: OVERT MANIPULATION

Months pass, and Jimmy's grip on the social dynamics of the school tightens. He operates quietly, almost methodically, turning several classmates against the student he is fixated on. Through whispers and insinuations, he spreads rumors, carefully crafting a narrative that paints her in a negative light. Presenting himself as the voice of reason, Jimmy frames his actions as a defense of shared values, all while undermining her reputation. Jimmy has come out from behind the curtain.

In class discussions, he challenges her assertions, but always under the guise of expressing "honest concerns" about her behavior. To an outsider, it seems like typical high school banter—a spirited debate among peers. But for those paying closer attention, there is a calculated edge to his words. Each comment is strategically designed to provoke doubt, making it appear as if he is merely looking out for the best interests of the group while subtly shifting the tides against her.

Despite his manipulations, Jimmy still appears to be a good kid in the eyes of his teachers. They notice his struggles, certainly, but they chalk them up to the typical tumult of teenage life, assuming he is simply going through a rough patch. No one suspects the depth of his frustration; his actions are cloaked in a veneer of reasonableness that obscures the underlying hostility.

Internally, however, Jimmy transforms. His focus shifts from mere frustration to a cold, deliberate strategy. He is no longer content to hide in the shadows; he fully embraces the role of an active discreditor, reveling in the power he feels as he orchestrates the social narrative.

Each day, he finds new ways to strengthen his influence, whether through group chats or casual hallway conversations. He ensures he's always around when others bring up the targeted student, subtly planting seeds of doubt and reinforcing the negative stories he spreads. As he becomes more invested in this role, he loses sight of the values he once held dear, letting

Chapter 21

his vendetta take precedence over the friendships he risks damaging in the process. He proclaims that his victim is an enemy of her own community (those she likes, loves and respect and with whom she want to be liked, loved and respected in return). She feels the weight of his aggression but hesitates to speak out, fearing the growing number of students aligned against her and doubting that adults, who view Jimmy as "a good kid who wouldn't do such a thing," would take her concerns seriously.

His classmates, caught in the web of his influence, find themselves drawn into the drama, some eagerly participating in the gossip while others remain unsure of their stance. Yet, Jimmy's charm and charisma make it easy for them to overlook the undercurrents of manipulation at play. As the lines between right and wrong blur, Jimmy's internal struggle becomes overshadowed by his newfound sense of power, leading him down a darker path that few can anticipate.

COMMENTARY

By now, Jimmy's aggression has shifted from covert manipulation to overt action. While he isn't yelling or directly confronting his target, he is strategically undermining her without raising alarms. To his teachers, Jimmy appears to be a typical teenager; his occasional challenges in class seem harmless, even constructive. They don't suspect that he is orchestrating a social campaign to isolate and discredit his peer. His calm demeanor masks the deeper aggression driving his actions, as he plays the long game to ruin her reputation.

As Jimmy's manipulation continues unnoticed, he becomes more strategic, carefully choosing when and where to act. During group projects or casual conversations, he plants seeds of distrust about the female student's integrity, framing her as untrustworthy. His classmates, unaware of his motives, begin to internalize these ideas, distancing themselves from the target and confirming Jimmy's influence over their opinions.

With growing confidence, Jimmy's actions become bolder. He starts to speak out more openly, claiming that the student isn't who she appears to be and hinting at fabricated issues. His aggression has shifted from passive resentment to active sabotage. To the untrained eye, it seems like typical high school drama, but those who know what to look for can see Jimmy is on a dangerous path.

As his fixation deepens, Jimmy's distorted thinking intensifies, leading him to feel justified in his actions. His internal narrative reinforces the belief that the student deserves his treatment. With his aggression becoming more overt, he increasingly neglects his personal responsibility for the consequences. He no longer views himself as merely venting frustration; he sees himself on a mission, driven by a sense of justified vengeance to take down his peer by any means necessary.

Without CAPS or an early intervention system, Jimmy's behavior continues unchecked. His teachers, friends, and classmates fail to recognize the growing danger. Each day, his Cognitive Aggression matures, becoming more dangerous. While he hasn't yet acted on his impulses to cause harm, the escalating intensity of his manipulation and hostility suggests that it's only a matter of time before his aggression takes a more sinister turn. If no one intervenes, Jimmy's descent into violence seems inevitable.

STAGE 6: THREATS AND STALKING

One day, it happens. The student Jimmy has been fixated on receives an anonymous message through social media: "I know what you did. You'll pay for this." The message is vague yet threatening enough to make her feel uneasy. It lingers in her mind, twisting her thoughts into knots. A few days later, while walking home from school, she notices a figure shadowing her steps, an unfamiliar presence that sends a chill down her spine. Her instincts scream that something isn't right, and she quickens her pace, feeling the weight of dread settle heavily on her shoulders.

She confides in a close friend, her voice shaking as she recounts the message and the feeling of being followed. The friend immediately suspects Jimmy, recalling the whispers and rumors circulating about him. But without concrete evidence linking him to the threats, there's little they can do. The friend urges her to stay vigilant, but a sense of helplessness washes over them both.

Meanwhile, the school administration steps in, prompted by the student's growing anxiety. They conduct a brief inquiry, speaking with Jimmy about the allegations. However, he denies everything, maintaining his innocent facade with practiced ease. To them, he still appears to be a good kid who is simply struggling through a rough patch. There is no substantial proof

Chapter 21

to implicate him, and their conversation is little more than a formality, leaving the underlying tension unresolved.

COMMENTARY

As Jimmy schemes, he meticulously plots each step of his plan, searching for ways to escalate the tension without exposing himself to scrutiny. He feels a twisted sense of empowerment in the secrecy of his actions, relishing the adrenaline rush that comes with outsmarting those around him. The thrill of manipulation drives him deeper into his delusion, as the lines between right and wrong blur further. He convinces himself that his actions are not only justified but absolutely necessary to reclaim his lost dignity and sense of control over a life that feels increasingly out of his grasp.

What began as mere frustration has morphed into a dangerous game of psychological warfare. Jimmy positions himself as the puppet master, orchestrating interactions and events to unsettle his target. He thrives on the tension he creates, believing that each small act of intimidation serves a greater purpose in his quest for vengeance. This growing obsession with control and retribution distorts his perception of reality; he sees himself as a wronged hero, poised to restore balance in his world.

With each passing day, the stakes continue to rise. What was once a quiet resentment has escalated into a full-blown fixation, enveloping his thoughts and actions. He imagines the satisfaction of finally confronting his classmate, envisioning the power that will come with making her feel the same pain he has endured. The clock is ticking, and the tension is palpable, creating an atmosphere thick with anxiety and uncertainty. Those around him may sense something is amiss, but Jimmy's deceptive facade keeps them at bay, allowing him to operate in the shadows of their awareness.

Without the Critical Aggression Prevention System (CAPS) in place, this escalating behavior flies under the radar. While Jimmy has become a genuine threat, without clear evidence, and the absence of a proactive framework leaves him unchecked. Law enforcement might get involved if a crisis arises, but without concrete evidence of a direct threat, their ability to act is severely limited. The school, too, is caught in a reactive mode, responding to incidents rather than anticipating them.

Teachers and staff may notice subtle changes in Jimmy's behavior—his withdrawn demeanor, the chilling comments he makes—but without a structured system to guide their responses, these warning signs are often dismissed or misinterpreted. The lack of an early intervention system creates a dangerous environment where aggressive tendencies can fester and grow unnoticed. One of the great flaws in "Threat Assessment" is that it presupposes a threat! You are now reacting to a perceived threat.

As Jimmy becomes more entrenched in his dangerous mindset, the repercussions of his unchecked aggression threaten to spill over into violence. The situation becomes increasingly volatile, with Jimmy standing on the precipice of a catastrophic conclusion. This unsettling reality highlights the urgent need for systems like CAPS, which are designed to recognize early signs of aggression and intervene before situations spiral out of control. Without such measures, individuals like Jimmy can continue their descent into darkness, leaving behind a trail of fear and devastation in their wake.

STAGE 7: THE CRISIS PHASE: ANONYMOUS THREATS

A month later, the situation takes a dramatic turn. One afternoon, the student Jimmy has been fixating on opens her locker to find an envelope shoved inside. Her heart races as she pulls it out, noticing the handwriting is jagged and hurried. Inside is a note that reads: "I know where you live. You'll be sorry." The message is direct, unmistakable, and terrifying, sending chills down her spine. What began as simmering frustration and social manipulation has now escalated into something far more dangerous—a blatant threat that feels like an act of terror.

The school administration is immediately alerted to the situation. They spring into action, reviewing the surveillance footage from the hallway near the lockers. The evidence is clear and damning—Jimmy is captured on camera slipping the envelope into her locker, a calculated act that seals his role in this escalation.

For the targeted student, the reality of the situation sinks in. She is terrified, feeling like a prisoner in her own school. Thoughts race through her mind as she questions the level of protection the school can provide. What is the responsibility of the school in ensuring her safety? Will they take further measures to protect her and her family from this escalating threat?

Chapter 21

Unfortunately, when the administration responds, the answer is disappointing. They offer only sympathy and a promise of a week or two of increased security patrols around the school. After that, it's left to her and her family to navigate the fallout on their own, feeling vulnerable and exposed.

The lack of adequate support leaves her feeling isolated and fearful. She wonders whether the school fully comprehends the gravity of the situation. Each day becomes a battle against her anxiety as she walks through the hallways, scanning for any sign of Jimmy or his friends. The shadow of his threat looms over her, transforming what should be a safe space into a source of dread.

At home, the tension escalates. She shares the news with her family, who react with a mix of anger and concern. They discuss the implications of the threat, weighing their options. Should they report the incident to the police? What if the school fails to act? Each discussion heightens her anxiety, as she grapples with the reality of needing to protect herself and her loved ones from someone she once considered just another classmate.

As the days pass, the atmosphere becomes charged with fear and uncertainty. The supportive friends who once rallied around Jimmy are now caught in a moral dilemma, torn between their loyalty to him and the unsettling realization of his escalating aggression. They begin to question whether their support for him has contributed to the cycle of intimidation, leading to a growing sense of unease within their social circle.

Jimmy, on the other hand, feels an intoxicating sense of power as he perceives himself as the orchestrator of this fear. The adrenaline rush fuels his actions, pushing him to further distances of hostility. He believes he's justified in his vendetta, convincing himself that the threat was merely a means to an end, a way to reclaim his sense of control.

COMMENTARY

Stage 7 marks the beginning of the Crisis Phase, where operational planning takes shape. What was once just ideation and theoretical in Stage 6 has now turned into action, as Jimmy moves to test his mental hypothesis. Emboldened by the steady support of his friends, he shifts from passive complaints to overt intimidation. No longer satisfied with simply undermining the targeted student socially, he now actively threatens her safety. This represents a critical escalation in his behavior, moving from psychological manipulation to a tangible and alarming threat.

The situation has become a powder keg, teetering on the brink of violence. The student's life is irrevocably altered, now overshadowed by Jimmy's aggression. With the stakes higher than ever, the potential for an even darker outcome looms ominously on the horizon.

The school recognizes the seriousness of the situation, yet even with law enforcement involved, their options are limited. They can talk to Jimmy and perhaps issue a warning, but such measures are unlikely to change his trajectory. Despite the gravity of his threats, he hasn't committed any actions that would warrant legal intervention.

In some states, such as Florida, laws like the Baker Act allow for a 72-hour hold if someone poses a threat to themselves or others. However, this is only a temporary fix. After those 72 hours, Jimmy could easily return to school, still fixated on his obsession. A restraining order might be issued, but for someone like Jimmy, whose fixation runs deep, a legal document alone won't deter him from his dangerous path.

Moreover, 21 states have enacted some form of Red Flag Laws, allowing for the temporary confiscation of weapons, but this process requires judicial approval, complicating matters further. There are two critical weaknesses in these laws. First, mental health or psychological evaluations can be overly subjective and often unreliable. Second, even when a judge approves the confiscation of weapons, they are typically seized for only 14 days before being returned. In cases like Jimmy's, where his determination and fixation are evident, this limited timeframe is unlikely to mitigate the risk of further escalation.

Without a Critical Aggression Prevention System (CAPS) in place, this crisis phase unfolds unchecked. Had CAPS been implemented earlier, Jimmy's escalating behavior could have been identified and addressed on numerous occasions well before reaching this critical point. A Certified Aggression Manager would have intervened long before Jimmy's threats became tangible, diffusing the situation before it posed a genuine threat. But without early intervention, aggression has spiraled out of control, leaving the victim in peril and everyone else scrambling for effective solutions.

STAGE 8: MAKING PLANS ACTIONABLE

At Stage Eight, Jimmy's aggression has transformed into a deeply entrenched form of Cognitive Aggression, marking a significant shift from the primal impulses that once characterized his behavior. His intent to inflict harm has matured into unwavering resolve, embodied in a chilling calmness that signals his ominous intentions. This eerie composure is reflected in the "thousand-yard stare" or "dead eyes," signs of complete emotional detachment that indicate a dangerous level of disconnection from reality.

In this state, Jimmy displays no fear, hesitation, or remorse. His body language reveals a chilling emotional detachment, signaling he has entered a psychological space fraught with danger. This dissociation enables him to plan without the constraints of empathy or moral conflict, focusing intently on his objective. His fixation on retribution sharpens his thoughts, making them methodical and precise. Each detail of his plan is carefully calculated, reflecting a level of premeditation that underscores the gravity of his intentions. He is prepared to sacrifice everything—his future, relationships, and even, if necessary, his life—yet his desire to survive remains intact. Driven by a cold, calculated need for vengeance, Jimmy is fully consumed, intent on fulfilling his mission at any cost.

This readiness to confront consequences complicates Jimmy's motivations. He has transitioned from merely wishing for revenge to actively seeking it, creating a paradox in his psyche. While he yearns for justice and validation, he also wants to survive the confrontation, leading him to strategize carefully to achieve his goals without falling victim to the fallout of his actions. This duality renders his aggression perilous; he is no longer just reacting but executing a plan with chilling precision.

As Jimmy becomes consumed by his thoughts, he isolates himself from any lingering connections to his former self or moral compass. His interactions with others become devoid of genuine connection, viewing relationships solely through the lens of utility. This isolation deepens his detachment, leaving him fixated on his target while disconnected from the emotional consequences of his planned actions.

COMMENTARY

Jimmy's transformation at Stage Eight serves as a stark reminder of the dangers of unchecked aggression and the human capacity to rationalize harmful behavior. This highlights the critical need for intervention at earlier stages of aggression escalation. Recognizing signs of Cognitive Aggression—such as chilling calmness and emotional detachment—provides vital opportunities for prevention and support. Without timely intervention, individuals like Jimmy can spiral deeper into aggression, leading to tragic outcomes for themselves and others.

This transformation is not merely individual but reflects a universal expression of advanced Cognitive Aggression. Regardless of background, those in Stage Eight will display the same vacant, detached look—a warning sign of perilous escalation. Recognizing this blank expression offers a crucial chance for intervention, enabling peers, teachers, or authorities to take action before the situation intensifies.

As Jimmy meticulously plans his actions, his goal transcends mere confrontation. He seeks to leave a lasting impact and make his classmate "pay" for perceived wrongs. His thoughts are cold and calculated, ensuring his attack will be swift and devastating. Although his primary objective is harm, Jimmy also intends to survive, showing that he is not driven by blind rage but by a calculated, consuming intent.

At this stage, Jimmy has reached what we call the "Moment of Commitment," the critical point where an assailant decides to act—akin to drawing a weapon with the intent to shoot. From the moment this decision is made, there is typically only a two-second window before the first shot is fired. No security officer or law enforcement (SRO) can reliably arrive in just two seconds, meaning that, in this instant, the target is entirely on their own. When law enforcement does arrive, they will follow Active Shooter Response Training, stepping over the dead, dying, and wounded to neutralize the shooter. This response, while understandable, is a reactive approach to a crisis that CAPS is designed to prevent. By intervening before the Moment of Commitment, CAPS provides a reliable means to address aggression before it reaches this tragic and horrific tipping point.

The easygoing, responsible boy his family and friends once knew has vanished, replaced by someone wholly absorbed by his obsession. Jimmy's life now centers around the revenge he feels entitled to exact, leaving

Chapter 21

behind school, hobbies, and close relationships. Friends and family, blinded by memories of the "quiet, reliable kid," dismiss his dark comments as harmless venting, failing to see he has crossed a line and is waiting for the right moment to act.

Without a Critical Aggression Prevention System (CAPS) in place, these warning signs can go unnoticed. A Certified Aggression Manager would have recognized Jimmy's subtle behavioral shifts—his isolation, darkening comments, and obsessive focus—intervening before he reached this dangerous threshold. Now, fully engulfed by his obsession, he is poised to strike. The stakes have never been higher, underscoring the urgent need for awareness and early intervention to prevent such tragedies.

STAGE 9: THE FINAL ACT

The day has come, and Jimmy has made his decision. As he walks to school, his mind is clear, his military-style jacket zipped tight, hands buried in his pockets. In his backpack, he carries what he believes will be his final act of retribution. He has one target in mind—her. To Jimmy, this student is the architect of his suffering, and today, he will ensure she pays. In his mind, she's to blame for everything, and now he's determined she'll experience the pain she's caused him.

With years of hunting experience and familiarity with firearms, Jimmy feels confident he can execute his plan. His objective is straightforward: confront her at her locker and make sure she knows she won't escape his wrath. He isn't thinking about what might follow; to him, everything else fades into the background. Convinced that he's already lost everything, he sees this as his one chance to be remembered, even if it's for something horrific. Jimmy knows that once he pulls the trigger, the school's SROs will be on the scene within minutes. He recalls from Active Shooter Training that they'll be ready to use lethal force, but he's unfazed. To him, this is like a video game—he'll engage them, they'll return fire, and it will end with his death. Suicide by cop.

At this point, Jimmy has reached the final stage of aggression. His mind and body are fully committed to his course of action. People at this stage—those willing to sacrifice everything for a cause—undergo a profound transformation. Their demeanor loses all vitality, becoming what is often described as the "thousand-yard stare" or "dead eyes." It's not just a blank face; his entire body language is lifeless, as if he has already accepted his fate.

His eyes are vacant, his movements mechanical. The boy who once cared about school, his friends, and his future is gone, replaced by someone entirely disconnected from his own well-being. This expression, recognizable to Certified Aggression Managers and Aggression First Observers, is a critical warning sign that intervention is urgently needed. Even at this last stage, there remains a narrow window to step in.

Again, this is about preventing violence, not creating it. Recognizing this transformation underscores a vital truth: it is not instinctual for one human to attack another. For someone like Jimmy to follow through with an attack, they must first disconnect, depersonalize, and reduce their target to an object, allowing them to justify harm. At the 9th Stage, however, aggression goes beyond merely disconnecting from the victim; individuals at this stage also disconnect from their own well-being. This profound detachment creates a chilling sense of calm, enabling a terrorist, for instance, to blow themselves up with their own children in the back seat. This is what makes the 9th Stage Cognitive Aggressor so lethal—their calmness in the face of destruction, having fully severed their attachment to their own life as well as the lives of others.

Jimmy's detachment from his own survival makes him exceptionally dangerous, fixated solely on carrying out his plan without regard for the consequences. His aggression has become a mission, trapping both him and his target in a lose/lose scenario. His eerie calm and focus signal that he is prepared to execute his final act, disregarding his life and anyone else's. It is murder-suicide in its purest form—an irreversible, self-destructive act where both he and his victim are bound to perish.

However, this tragic outcome is preventable. With systems like CAPS and trained professionals who can recognize these warning signs early, intervention could redirect individuals like Jimmy before they reach this point. By identifying and addressing aggression at its earliest stages, we can prevent such crises from escalating into irreversible acts, safeguarding lives and fostering safer environments for everyone involved.

Chapter 21

COMMENTARY

This moment reflects the chilling calm often seen in individuals who have reached Stage 9 of aggression, serving as a sobering reminder of how unchecked aggression can escalate into something unimaginable. Jimmy's journey from mere frustration to full-blown violence didn't happen overnight; it was a gradual, insidious escalation marked by numerous access points where timely intervention could have made a profound difference. The warning signs were evident: disconnection from reality, simmering resentment, subtle manipulation, and finally, overt threats. Yet, no one intervened, and now, tragically, it's too late.

This stark reality underscores the critical importance of systems like the Critical Aggression Prevention System (CAPS), which are designed to identify early signs of aggression and prevent situations like Jimmy's from spiraling into violence. CAPS could have detected his increasing hostility long before he reached this final, tragic stage.

The system operates on the premise that aggression often follows a discernible trajectory. Certified Aggression Managers are trained to recognize the early warning signs of escalating aggression, allowing them to intervene proactively. They are equipped with the tools and knowledge to assess behavior patterns, facilitate conversations, and provide necessary support before the situation escalates further.

Yet, even in the final moments, when it seems all hope is lost, there remains a glimmer of opportunity to avert disaster. By recognizing the chilling calm that accompanies an individual at this dangerous stage, those around them can still take action. The responsibility lies not just with professionals but with peers, educators, and community members to be vigilant and aware of the signs of aggression. It may only be moments, but with CAPS you have an opportunity to get out in front of this horrific Moment of Commitment and prevent it from happening.

Education and awareness are vital in fostering environments where individuals feel empowered to seek help and where supportive measures can be enacted before a situation escalates beyond control. By creating a culture of vigilance, we can work together to identify those in distress and address their needs before it's too late. If we learn from Jimmy's tragic story, we can better equip ourselves to recognize the subtle shifts in behavior that precede acts of violence, ensuring that we take action before it becomes a matter of life and death.

Conclusion: A Cautionary Tale

As this story illustrates, the subtle changes in Jimmy's disposition over time are often overlooked or ignored by those around him—teachers, friends, and family alike. His journey highlights how escalating aggression can affect any student, irrespective of their background. Jimmy's transformation from frustration to violence serves as a stark reminder of the tragic consequences that can arise from unchecked aggression.

But can this really happen? If you've ever wondered whether simple frustration can escalate into extreme, even lethal violence, Jimmy's narrative provides a compelling answer. Although fictional, his story closely mirrors real-life events that we have witnessed—and continue to witness—with alarming frequency in schools across the nation. In virtually all these cases, the perpetrators exhibited warning signs—disconnection, fixation, and escalating hostility—that went unnoticed or were dismissed by those around them. Sadly, Jimmy's experience is not unique; it reflects the path many young people follow when their frustrations remain unaddressed.

As Jimmy's aggression intensified, it went largely unnoticed by his teachers, friends, and family, who rationalized his behavior as typical teenage angst. This dismissal allowed his emotional turmoil to fester, and as he progressed along the aggression continuum, his thoughts grew darker and more sinister. This transformation made him increasingly dangerous, ultimately culminating in an unimaginable act of violence. His story serves as a cautionary tale, demonstrating the devastating outcomes that can result from failing to recognize early warning signs.

Once perceived as a responsible, quiet student, Jimmy morphed into someone capable of horrific acts due to the lack of intervention in his escalating aggression. However, systems like the Critical Aggression Prevention System (CAPS) exist to change this narrative. CAPS is designed to identify, intervene, and address the warning signs of aggression before they spiral out of control. By fostering an environment where early intervention is prioritized, we can significantly reduce the risk of tragic outcomes.

Remember, only when we can measure something can we truly manage it. The implementation of systems like CAPS offers us a critical opportunity to recognize the precursors to aggressive incidents, enabling us to intervene before it's too late. By being vigilant and proactive, we can help prevent the devastating consequences of unchecked aggression, ensuring a safer environment for all students.

A School at Risk: Preventing the Rise of Violence through Early Detection

As we navigate the complex anatomy of school shooters like Jimmy, it is crucial to recognize that schools should be sanctuaries of physical, mental, and emotional safety—places designed for learning, growth, and development. The alarming rise in school violence poses a significant threat to the social and academic climate inherent in these environments. However, this threat can be mitigated through early detection of aggressive behaviors. Ignoring the warning signs is a perilous choice that risks transforming our schools into unsafe breeding grounds for unchecked frustration and anger.

Reflecting on Jimmy's journey, it becomes evident that his aggression could have been managed and redirected if someone had noticed the early signs and intervened appropriately. His progressive disconnection from peers, fixation on a specific classmate, and increasing manipulation pointed to deeper issues that demanded attention. Unfortunately, without a system like CAPS in place, these critical signs were overlooked, no action was taken, and tragedy inevitably followed.

We possess the power to prevent tragedies like Jimmy's from occurring. By implementing systems that identify early precursors of aggression, such as CAPS, and by providing support to students before their frustrations escalate into violence, we can protect both potential victims and aggressors. Preventing aggression not only safeguards against violence but also enhances a school's overall productivity and sense of community. By fostering a culture of trust and support, we can create environments where students collaborate to achieve their fullest potential, rather than being divided by conflict. Schools can become incubators of trust, where conflicts are managed constructively, and where students feel safe expressing themselves.

As we conclude, let's reaffirm that the safety of our schools hinges on our commitment to early detection and intervention. While the Critical Aggression Prevention System (CAPS) does not claim that a student in Stage 3 is guaranteed to escalate to Stage 8 or 9, it seeks to highlight the undeniable connection between these stages in the absence of intervention—an alarming pattern we have witnessed all too frequently. The progression from low levels of aggression to higher, more dangerous ones is real, and tragically, it is often only in hindsight that we can see where early intervention might have made a significant difference.

The goal of CAPS is straightforward: identify students on this perilous path early, engage with them, and redirect their aggression before it escalates into bullying, harassment, physical violence, or worse. When students are driven by aggressive impulses, they lose their ability to cooperate, respect boundaries, and find common ground. By measuring and understanding aggression in its early stages, we can prevent it from becoming endemic to school culture, allowing students to thrive both socially and academically. In doing so, we avert both personal and societal harm, creating safer, more supportive environments for everyone. With the right tools and a proactive approach, we can ensure that tragedies like Jimmy's remain stories, not realities. Together, we can forge a future where our schools truly embody safety and support for all.

Preventing Tragedy: A Legal Responsibility?

Because attendance is mandatory in secondary schools, teachers and staff carry a unique and profound obligation to create a safe environment for every student. Governed by the principle of "in loco parentis," educators and school administrators assume the role of surrogate parents, taking on the responsibility for the physical and emotional well-being of the students in their care. This duty extends beyond mere ethics; it is grounded in legal obligations as well.

While schools generally enjoy immunity under the doctrine of state sovereign immunity, this legal shield can be breached if it can be shown that teachers and staff have been grossly negligent in their duty of care. If a school fails to address early warning signs of aggression or ignores behaviors that could escalate into violence, it risks liability for neglecting its ethical responsibility to protect students. Gross negligence—such as knowingly overlooking or dismissing clear threats or behavioral

Chapter 21

concerns—exposes both students and staff to unnecessary risks and undermines the trust that parents place in schools to act in their children's best interests.

The implications of this responsibility are far-reaching. Schools are not just places of learning; they are communities where students should feel safe and supported. When aggression goes unaddressed, it not only jeopardizes individual students but can also create a climate of fear that disrupts the entire learning environment. Teachers and staff must remain vigilant, recognizing that their actions—or inactions—can have significant consequences.

Implementing tools like the Critical Aggression Prevention System (CAPS) can be instrumental in helping schools fulfill this responsibility. CAPS offers a structured framework for the early detection of aggressive behaviors, enabling educators to intervene proactively before issues escalate into violence. By utilizing scientifically backed methods for identifying warning signs, schools can effectively manage aggression while respecting privacy regulations.

The benefits of adopting CAPS extend beyond mere compliance with legal obligations; they foster a culture of safety and trust within the school community. When students, parents, and educators know that there is a system in place to identify and address aggression early, it cultivates a sense of security that enhances the overall educational experience. This proactive approach not only helps prevent potential tragedies but also reinforces the school's commitment to nurturing a positive and inclusive environment.

Ultimately, the responsibility of ensuring a safe learning environment lies with everyone in the school community. By prioritizing the well-being of students through vigilant observation and intervention, educators can fulfill their ethical and legal obligations, creating a school atmosphere where all students can thrive academically and emotionally.

www.ingramcontent.com/pod-product-compliance
Lightning Source LLC
LaVergne TN
LVHW021958060526
838201LV00048B/1616